# Fed by Grace

Titus 2

# Inspiring Recipes
# by Inspiring Women

Titus II ladies present their best family recipes.
All proceeds of sales of this cookbook to be used for their
philanthropic projects.

First Edition
© Copyright 12/1/2010 Titus II Group
ISBN 978-0-9830094-0-5

Photography & Graphic Design by Kelly Clower
Blue Skies Design, LLC

# Contents

# Foreword

Everyone enjoys eating! Many of the memories that we have in our lives come from time around the dinner table with both family and friends. There is something special about sharing a meal together. Think about it. I believe Jesus understood this also. Take a moment and examine the number of times Jesus used mealtime as a time to teach, to share, and to listen. He found that many "teachable moments" can be discovered as people eat together! I believe that He wants us to do the same!

This cookbook is designed to give you some of the best recipes you will find anywhere! This book has been put together by one of our small groups at Lakeside Church, who wants to serve our community. These are people who have a desire to find those "teachable moments" and use them as we try to live a life which reflects the nature and character of Jesus.

I hope and pray that you will enjoy the recipes you find listed here as not just another good "dish", but you will also use these recipes to bring family and friends together.
God Bless!

Lee Ross
Senior pastor, Lakeside Church

Everyone talks about wanting to make a difference in their community, but so few of us find practical ways to do so. The Titus 2* ladies group at Lakeside Church has found a way to make a real difference. This cookbook is a collection of great recipes that will enable families to share meals and memories together. Connecting people is a foundational purpose for us at Lakeside Church and this book can be used to help connect people with their family and friends.

Seeing lives changed is another purpose in which God has lead Lakeside Church to be an active participant. In light of that, the proceeds from this cookbook will be used to help the church respond to the immediate needs of individuals and families in our community. Not only will we get a chance to tell those in need about Jesus, this cookbook will enable us to show them the love of Jesus in practical ways.

We greatly appreciate your partnership in helping to meet the needs of our community and we pray that God will bless you and your family as you share your meals and your lives together.

Dream big,
**Jay Thompson**
Pastor of Community and Connection
Lakeside Church


*Titus 2:3-5 (HCSB)
*"In the same way, older women are to be reverent in behavior, not slanderers, not addicted to much wine. They are to teach what is good, so that they may encourage the young women to love their husbands and children, to be sensible, pure, good homemakers, and submissive to their husbands, so that God's message will not be slandered."*

# Introduction to Titus 2

Hi, I am **Maggie McLendon**, the facilitator of the Titus 2 Group and I would like to introduce the Titus 2 Group to all the readers of this cookbook. We hope all of you will enjoy this cookbook and the recipes we have chosen to share with you. We each selected favorites that we have tried and tested over the years. Our goal is to be successful in giving you a cook-book of good recipes to treasure. We appreciate you purchasing this cookbook and assure you that this will help us accomplish our goal of supporting the many philanthropic projects which we are involved in. We want to find ways to "walk across the room" and touch someone else who is in need. This can be a telephone call, a helping hand, a basket of groceries when there is no food in the pantry, supporting a child to have school clothing or providing funds for necessary medical needs to those that have no insurance.

The purpose of our group is to share in Christian love with many young ladies in our church that need a fellowship where they can have a day out from the usual routine, enjoy some good food, share how God is working in each of their lives, needing prayer for special needs and just knowing that we all share a common bond of love. We could be considered a "sisterhood" of Christian love and fellowship. We are learning how to be accountable within our group and to set the example of love for others.

I live in Reynolds Plantation, Greensboro, Ga., with my husband, Harold. He is a retired physician from Carrollton, Ga. and I am a retired business owner and interior designer from Savannah, Ga., and Hilton Head, S.C. We have a combined family of five children and twelve grandchildren. In 2005 we moved to the Oconee Area from Hilton Head, S.C. We have grown to love this spot of heaven in Georgia, especially all the friendly people we have met. We have families in the Atlanta area and can visit often. We enjoy a wonderful and warm fellowship in our Lakeside Church, where the mission is loving God, changing lives and connecting people.

My life has been blessed in many different ways, through some highs and through some lows, but the greatest blessing I have enjoyed is knowing Christ and sharing a personal relationship with him. As I am traveling through my golden years , I cherish this opportunity to share my life story and be a mentor to this Titus 2 group of ladies. I want to give a big "thanks" to Nancy Brooks and Barbara Williams for being my sidekicks. They exude love and compassion for all of us and both happen to be wonderful wives, mothers, and cooks and most of all, they are wonderful Christian mentors.

**Karen Alley** is married to Trey, the real Gourmet Chef, who cooks with ingredients from the "Trey Food Pyramid" which consists of mayonnaise, butter, sour cream and sugar. Can you believe, Karen blames his cooking for making her fat. She enjoys reading, watching movies, going for walks and cooking when she is in the mood and has access to the kitchen. Karen says she was pleasantly surprised to find she had an instant "Sisterhood" with the Titus 2 girls.

**Amy Andraszek** and her husband, Robert, have been married for 10 years. They have been blessed with two young sons, Jared and Raymond. In no way does Amy profess to be an outstanding cook, as her husband suffers from severe food allergies and she has to be careful what and how to cook. However she does appreciate good cooking and takes advantage of the good cooking of others as often as possible. She submitted recipes she has enjoyed over the years and it is her hope you will enjoy them.

**Audrey Beals** moved to the Lake Oconee area in 2006 with her husband and two children. She said it was God's answer to a prayer. Her husband, Doug, had always wanted to live at Lake Oconee and she wanted to move out of the metro Atlanta area and raise her kids in the country . They are now happily settled in this beautiful part of Georgia. She says that being part of the Titus 2 group has been one of the greatest blessings she has received since moving here. The wonderful mentorship and great friendships within the group have filled a deep need she had felt for many years. She fills her days homeschooling her children, leading the local home school group she started, driving her children to various activities, as well as running a small business from home. She places God, her husband, children and her relationships at the top of her list of priorities. One of her favorite verses is Proverbs 3:5-7 "Trust in the Lord with all your heart and lean not on your own understanding, In all your ways acknowledge Him and he shall direct your path. Be not wise in your own eyes, fear the Lord and shun evil."

**Nancy Brooks** is one of the seasoned members of the group. She and her husband, Bob, have been married 48 years this August. Living on Oconee lake has been fun-- pulling in fish from their dock and having the children and grandchildren come to enjoy all kinds of water activities each summer, making many family memories. Nancy and Bob are very involved in their Lakeside Church. She loves being in her kitchen cooking up something for the family, friends or making a meal to take to the sick. Nancy tries to keep a cookie jar full of homemade cookies for Bob, who could be called the cookie monster! She also enjoys motorcycle riding with Bob, decorating the home, sewing, reading and working on projects together. She feels the Titus 2 group has given her a chance to share her story and offer encouragement and support for them in their daily walk. She and Bob are also mentors for young couples and young singles in our church.

**Damaris Callaway** has been married to Lynn for over 18 years. They were high school sweethearts and still enjoy sharing their lives together. They are the proud parents of two teenagers, Phillip and Kourtni. She and Lynn enjoy sharing their lives together with their children, giving them a good Christian foundation which to help them on their journey in life. Damaris is employed as the Lakeside Church Office Coordinator. She feels thankful to be part of the Titus II group and describes these ladies as awesome! Although she believes she is not the best cook in the group she thinks she has been good enough to convince her family that "mom can cook". A scripture that Damaris likes to share is: 2 Timothy 1:7-- "For God has not given us a spirit of fear, but of power and love and sound mind."

Tam Cole is married to a "wonderful guy", Tim. They have three sons. The first two came along early in their marriage and much later they were blessed with another son. Since the family has accepted Christ into their lives, they have all blossomed under His love. She has chosen to home school her youngest son even though she never thought she could walk out of her comfort zone and teach . Because of her rather sheltered and reserved life, Tam says she was reluctant to join the Titus 2 Group. At first, she definitely felt out of her comfort zone, but the ladies have made this transition more pleasant than she could have asked for. She thanks God for being a part of this group, which has provided her with what she needed without her even knowing it. She says, "when our hearts are focused on Christ, all things are possible".

Doris McAfee and her husband, Ken from Arizona, moved to Greensboro, Ga. two years ago. She and Ken met while working for the Department of Defense in Washington, D.C., a career which spanned 22 years. They enjoy their combined family of 7 children and 11 grandchildren. Her love affair with gourmet cooking began shortly after she and Ken started dating 12 years ago. She says each day is a new opportunity for her to show her love for Ken through her love for cooking.

Sharon Royal Minchey has lived in Eatonton, Ga. all of her life. She feels this is just where she always belongs. She loves her surroundings, and is happy to be raising her kids in a small town environment. She and Jason have been married for 14 years and they have two daughters. She has a full time job but also finds time to be involved in prison ministry, Pathway to Freedom, as well as pursuing further education in Addiction Counseling. Shannon is the joy of our group, as she is so open and radiating with love for others. She feels so blessed to share some of her life with the outstanding ladies of Titus 2.

April Murray is "the baby of the group". She is the youngest member of the Titus 2 Group and the only childless one (not for long, God willing). She has been married to Chase for 1½ years and they are a very active couple in the Lakeside Church. She says God has truly blessed her to be part of the Titus 2 group, especially at the beginning stages of her marriage. The older ladies have a lot of wisdom to pass on, and she likes to think she keeps the group "young". She says the sisterhood of ladies has been a joy and a blessing already to her. She feels she is learning a lot by listening and loving, making her feel so blessed.

**Robin Plessl** is happily married to Gary and they are blessed with one son, Danny. They only recently moved to Georgia and love the southern hospitality and most certainly their new found church family at Lakeside in Lake Oconee. She is most pleased to be a member of the Titus 2 ladies group and to join in this service project to develop a cookbook. She is very interested in fitness and maintaining a healthy lifestyle that includes healthy eating choices. Working full time does not always allow ample time to make extravagant dinners. However, a concerted effort is made to insure the food prepared is both delicious and nutritious.

**Deann Snipes** is blessed with 2 very active and unique boys, Gage & Cole who keep her life exciting and noisy. Deann enjoys doing things that require her to use her imagination and to think outside the box. She truly is a Southern girl who cannot wear white before Easter or after Labor day. A sassy new pair of shoes can make her day or even her week. She loves Grandma's fried chicken, Georgia Bulldog football, and the beauty that only the spring in the South can provide. In her life, she has faced many different challenges and it is through some of those challenges that she came to know many of the ladies in the group. She came to know the power of their prayers and the generosity of their hearts long before she had the pleasure of personally knowing them. Throughout her challenges, God has taught her many lessons, and one of the greatest is to find joy in every circumstance. A quote that seems to explain it simply: "We should consider every day lost in which we have not danced at least once." So, Deann says dance!

**Barbara Williams** feels she lucked out when she married Donald. He not only is "Mr. Fixit" but also loves to cook. They celebrated 50 years together in 2008, and God entrusted them with four children. Needless to say, she was a soccer mom plus. In the middle of raising their family, Donald went back to Veterinary School to get his D.V.M. Being an O.B. nurse, Barbara worked on her P.H.T. degree (Putting Hubby Thru). She enjoys family and friends, reading , flower arranging, singing, fishing and cooking. She enjoys animals and likes traveling to see God's great creation. Barbara competed in the Ohio Mrs. America Pageant and was required to furnish a Chicken recipe (which you will find in this cookbook). She feels honored that she was selected as Mrs. Congeniality. In 2003, they moved from the gulf coast of Florida to Lake Oconee, and became very active in their church, Lakeside. After the Titus 2 Group was started she was glad for the opportunity to mentor younger ladies.

**Kelly Clower** credits her culinary gifts to her very talented mother who loved to entertain family and friends in their Pennsylvania home. Kelly and her southern husband, Barry, now reside in Georgia with their slew of animals, including (at the moment) nine chickens, two horses, three cats and their dog, Mandy, who is pictured on the last page of this book.

# Acknowledgements

A special thanks to Kelly Clower for all the hard work she has done to bring this cookbook to fruition. She has served as our graphic designer, photographer, creative director and cover designer and has taken all of our favorite recipes and created an inspirational keepsake for you and your own families to enjoy.

A special thanks to Harold McLendon, who has put all of our recipes, descriptions and images in a typewritten format for the printer and publisher.  A special thanks to Trey and Karen Alley.  Karen has contributed her time to contact all the ladies for submitting their Bios and recipes.  Trey has guided us with much of his talents and taken the typewritten format and proceeded with the publication of the cookbook.  Pastor Jay Thompson of Lakeside has graciously provided his guidance and suggestions for publishing this outstanding cookbook.  A special thanks to Elaine Watson who contributed her editing skills in helping us to proofread all the cookbook material.  A special thanks to all the Titus 2 Group ladies for their tried and tested recipes.

Most of all we want to thank all of you who support us with your purchase of this cookbook.  We pray that you will enjoy every one that you will test and that you will find many of them to become one of your favorites.

"Bon appétit"
Maggie McLendon

# Appetizers

Appetizers, as we know them, were not common fare in the early days. There were nuts, including walnuts, hickory nuts, chestnuts and pecans which were locally grown from orchards or from the woods. Served at receptions were teas and coffee, also offered were chicken salad, cheese straws and biscuits as well as cakes and cookies. Today, appetizers comprise of a number of dishes with the use of fruits, vegetables and meats.

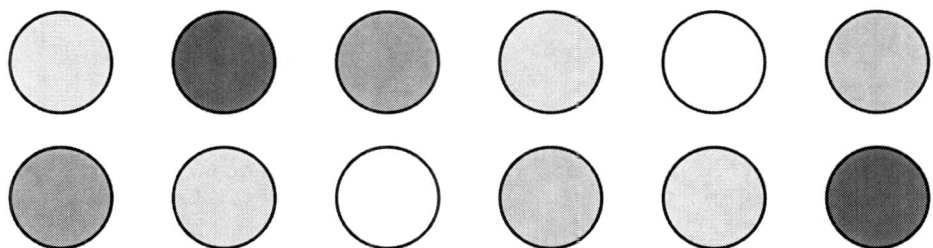

*Fed by Grace*

## Artichoke Dip

I   can artichokes (drained and mashed)
8   oz. shredded mozzarella cheese
1   cup parmesan cheese
1   cup mayo
½   grated onion
4   dabs of butter
Bread crumbs
Few dashes garlic powder

      Mix together the above and add to round 8" or 9" pan.
Sprinkle bread crumbs over top and add 4 dabs of butter to top.
Cook @ 350  degrees for 20 minutes.

*Maggie's granddaughter, Kristen, shared a few of her favorite recipes.  This dip is very delicious and she get raves every time it is served.*

*Researchers are finding out that artichokes can help reduce the risk of certain types of heart diseases, cancers and birth defects.*

## Artichoke Dip with Crab

2     14 oz. cans artichoke hearts
1     cup mayonnaise
1     cup grated parmesan cheese
½    lb. crab meat
Cayenne pepper to taste

     Drain artichoke hearts well. Chop and mash with fork or combine in food processor (do not puree too finely). Add mayonnaise, parmesan cheese, crab meat and seasoning. Bake in casserole dish at 350 degrees about 20 minutes until it is bubbly. Serve with crackers.

*Savannah natives will throw a party just to be able to serve this old and delicious favorite dip. The book, "In the Garden of Good and Evil", written about Savannah reveals a lot of history about this beautiful city including the Jim Williams' famous murder case. When Jim gave his famous "parties" to the chosen, this was always the most requested dish.*

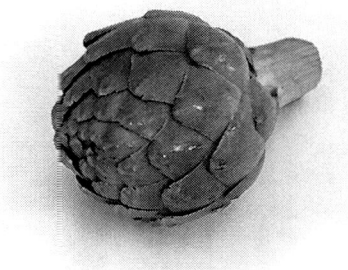

## <u>Cheese Ball</u>

2 tsp. Worcestershire sauce
2 8 oz. cream cheese at room temperature
2 cups shredded sharp cheddar cheese
1 tbsp. pimento
1 tbsp. chopped onion
1 tbsp. green onion
1 Tbsp green pepper
2 tsp. lemon juice
Pecans for topping

In mixer combine the cream cheese and cheddar cheese. Chop onion and green pepper in to small pieces. Add with all the rest of ingredients and mix. Add small amount of milk to thin if necessary. Shape into ball. Sprinkle with pecans, refrigerate for several hours, better if overnight. Serve with Ritz crackers.

*A friend gave Barbara this cheese ball recipe. It's easy to make and especially nice to have for Thanksgiving and Christmas holidays.*

## <u>Cheese Wedges</u>

1   25 oz. pkg. frozen uncooked biscuits, slight thawed
2   tbsp. butter, melted
1   cup grated sharp cheddar cheese or fresh parmesan cheese

      Preheat oven to 375 degrees.  Arrange biscuits on a cookie sheet, pressing each one to slightly flatten.  Cut into quarters.  Brush the tops with melted butter, then sprinkle with grated cheese.  Bake for 15 to 20 minutes, until golden.

*Biscuits are always enjoyed by the men folk.  "These make a hit every time they are served", Nancy.*

> Sometimes God has to put us flat on our back before we are looking up to Him.

# Fed by Grace

## Chicken-Cucumber Canapés

2    (8oz.) pkg. cream cheese, softened
¾    cup mayonnaise
3    cups diced cooked chicken
¾    cup peeled, seeded, diced cucumber
3    celery ribs, diced
½    cup diced bell pepper
6    green onions, chopped
1    tsp. garlic salt
½    tsp. salt
84  white or wheat sandwich bread slices (about 4 loaves)
Minced fresh parsley (optional)

      Stir together cream cheese and mayonnaise.  Stir in chicken and next 7 ingredients.  Cover and chill at least 4 hours.  Cut bread slices with assorted 2 1/2 –inch cutters, reserving trimmings for other uses.  Spread half of bread shapes with chicken mixture.  Top each with a matching bread shape.   Roll sandwich edges in parsley, if desired.  Yield: 7 dozen.

*A truly enjoyable make-ahead beginning!  They will be a hit at an afternoon tea buffet.  The parsley adds color as well as taste.*

*To keep sandwiches fresh, cover with a damp cloth.*

## Chinese Fried Walnuts

6   cups water
½   cup sugar
4   cups English walnuts

     Bring water to boil in large saucepan. Add nuts and return to boil. Cook 1 minute. Rinse nuts with hot running water and drain well. In large bowl stir nuts with sugar until dissolved. Heat 1 inch of salad oil to 350 degrees. Add ½ nuts and fry 5 minutes or until golden brown. Drain well and sprinkle with salt.

*"This is one of my favorite dishes to serve at a social gathering. You can't stop just with eating a few. Also try my "Orange Pecans" recipe." Karen.*

*Unsaturated fats found in walnuts and other nuts are effective in lowering heart problems and satisfying your hunger.*

## Crab Dip

8   oz. cream cheese
12  oz. fresh crabmeat
1   tbsp horseradish
1   tsp. Worchester sauce
1   tsp. milk
1   tsp. garlic
1   grated onion and juice
Pinch paprika

Mix all ingredients and top with slivered almonds. Bake at 350 degrees for 30 minutes. Serve with pita chips or crackers.

*Maggie shares this favorite crab recipe given to her by Mrs. Dot of Bluffton, S. C. She lived on the May river and always had fresh seafood for all of her cooking.*

*Mrs. Dot passed away recently and this recipe is shared with you in her memory.*

## **Crab Ring**

1 pkg. unflavored gelatin (dissolved in 3 tbsp. water)
1    cup finely chopped celery
½    cup chopped onions (green)
1    cup mayonnaise
1    8oz. package cream cheese (room temperature)
1    can drained crab
1    cup cold water
1    can of cream of mushroom soup

Mix first four ingredients together and set aside.  Dissolve gelatin in water.  Heat cream of mushroom soup and add dissolved gelatin to soup and stir until dissolved.  Add to other mixture and pour into lightly greased mold.  Then  refrigerate.

*At tastings, we found this appetizer to be equally delicious on tiny rounds of pumpernickel or on crostini.*

## Cucumber Sandwiches

1    large cucumber, peeled, seeded, and grated
1    (8 ounce) pkg. cream cheese, softened
1    tbsp. mayonnaise
1    small shallot, minced
¼   tsp. seasoned salt
1    (16 ounce) loaf sandwich bread
Garnish: cucumber slices

Drain cucumber well, pressing between layers of paper towels. Stir together cucumber and next 4 ingredients. Spread mixture evenly over half of bread slices. Top with remaining bread slices. Trim crusts from sandwiches, and cut in half diagonally. Garnish, if desired. Store sandwiches in an airtight container. Yield: 16 sandwiches .

*Maggie says this dainty sandwich doesn't stay around long when served. These are easy to make and easy to eat. Try them and you will agree.*

*Mix white and pumpernickel breads for interest.*

## Eggs Stuffed With Goat Cheese

6    large eggs, hard-boiled and peeled
3    tbsp. goat cheese
3    tbsp. mayonnaise
2    tbsp. chutney
2    tbsp. finely chopped pecans
2    tbsp. finely chopped celery
Salt and black pepper
Chopped parsley leaves, optional
Additional goat cheese and pecans, optional

Halve eggs lengthwise. Remove yolks and place in a small bowl. Mash yolks with fork and stir in goat cheese, mayonnaise, chutney, pecans and celery. Add salt and pepper, to taste. Fill egg whites evenly with yolk mixture. Garnish with parsley, goat cheese and pecans, if desired.

*Doris, who's known for being a super cook, says these are not your usual deviled eggs. Once you taste them, you'll love them.*

*If you are unsure of the freshness of your eggs, use the float test. Place in pot of hot water and if they do not sink, they are not fresh.*

## " Famous" Cheese Ring

1   lb. sharp cheddar cheese, grated
1   cup pecans, chopped
¾   cup mayonnaise
1   med. onion, grated
1   clove garlic, pressed
½   tsp. Tabasco
1   cup strawberry preserves

Combine all ingredients except preserves and mix well.  Chill.
Mold into ring.  Fill with strawberry preserves.  Serve with crackers
or chips.

*This delicious dish will get your gala holiday dinner off to an auspicious start.   This appetizer gets high marks for its visual appeal and richness of flavor...easy to make, a delight to serve and always enjoyed.*

## Fig Preserves Over Goat Cheese

8    halved dried figs
2    tbsp. butter
1    tsp. thyme
1    tbsp. balsamic vinegar
6    oz. goat cheese
Pinch of salt

      Remove stems from figs and place in sauce pan.  Cover with water and simmer 5 minutes.  Drain and cool.  Melt 1 tbsp. butter in skillet.  Add 1 cup thinly sliced onion and brown.  Stir in figs and 1 tsp. thyme and salt.  Cook 2 minutes.  Add 1 tbsp. balsamic vinegar.  Cook 2-3 minutes until glazed.  Place 6 oz. goat cheese in serving bowl.  Spoon mixture over.  Serve with crackers.

*This dish is very appealing….easy to make and a delight to serve. Maggie says you might better double the recipe as they go fast with fig lovers.*

## Fresh Fruit Dip

½  cup firmly packed brown sugar
1   (8oz.) package cream cheese, softened
1   cup sour cream
1   tsp. vanilla extract
1   cup frozen whipped topping, thawed

Beat brown sugar and cream cheese at medium speed with an electric mixer until smooth.  Add sour cream, and vanilla.  Beat until blended and smooth.  Fold in whipped topping.  Cover and chill 4 hours.  Serve with assorted fresh, seasonal fruit(s).

*This is delicious with apples as well as with most all fresh fruits such as strawberries and melons.*

*Remember an apple a day will keep the Doctor away.*

# Appetizers

## Glennville Onion Dip

1   8 oz.  shredded cheddar cheese
2   cups mayonnaise
2   cup chopped onions

Mix together.  Pour into a 1 quart greased baking dish.  In preheated oven, bake at 325 degrees for 50 minutes or until tender. Sprinkle 2 tbsp grated parmesan cheese on top when taken out of oven.

*Glennville, Ga. cooks feel their local grown onions are as good if not better than those famous "Vidalia Onions".  This recipe was shared by Dana Durrence, who has a large farm and grows many onions that are shipped all over the country.*

## Hawaiian Meatballs

1    pkg. frozen meatballs
2    (14 to 18 oz.) bottles ketchup
1    cup brown sugar
1    cup water
2    tsp. Worcestershire sauce
1    tsp. vinegar (white)
1    tsp. mustard
1    whole onion (for flavor)

Mix all ingredients together and place in Crockpot. Add meatballs and simmer for one hour (uncovered). Double the recipe for a crowd.

*Another favorite dish for the men folk. Easy and quick to prepare, and great to serve at a buffet or a covered dish get-together.*

## Hot Brie Cheese Dip

1   round Brie cheese
Any fruit preserves
Toasted walnuts
Crackers or baguettes

Cut off top of cheese and heat in microwave approximately one minute or until soft.  Spread fruit preserves over Brie.  Sprinkle toasted walnuts over top.  Serve with crackers or baguettes.

*A round of Brie, warmed and melted ---outrageous.  This dish  is easy to prepare and really delicious-- a little calls for more.*

## Mexican Dip

1    cup sour cream
1    cup mayonnaise
1    pkg. taco seasoning
6    roma tomatoes, chopped
1    bunch green onions, chopped
2    half cup cheese, grated

    Mix sour cream, Mayonnaise and taco seasoning together.  In a casserole dish layer sour cream mixture first, tomatoes, green onions and last top with cheese.  Chill 2 hours before serving.  Serve with tortilla chips.

*Shannon contends this is everyone's favorite.  It's especially popular with the teenagers.*

## Mozzarella Cheese Appetizer

    Equal parts of grated onion, fancy shredded mozzarella cheese, and mayonnaise.  Mix together and spread on white or brown bread.  Bake at 450 degrees until lightly brown on top.

*This is an easy recipe from Damaris.   These are quick to prepare and good to nibble on before you get serious about dinner.*

## Ms. Polly's Appetizer

1  pkg. chicken livers
1  pkg. bacon of any kind
1  pre-sprayed pan

Cut chicken livers in half and bacon. Wrap the liver with a bacon strip and put in a toothpick to hold it. Broil on high for about 10 minutes or until done.

*Tam shares this recipe from Ms. Polly, one of the finest cooks in our area. She shared her Christian love with all and was a very good role model for Tam.*

## Olive Spread

1 cup chopped green salad olives
½ cup mayonnaise
½ cup chopped pecans
8 oz. cream cheese
2 tbsp. olive juice
Pinch black pepper
Pinch hot sauce

Mix first 5 ingredients well. Add black pepper. Add Hot Sauce to taste. Serve with crackers.

*This recipe was given to DeAnn by her friend, Brenda Coker. It is a wonderful mixture of flavors, that is easy to whip up and is rather filling.*

*Olives are the very best source of good fats that are not saturated. Although not essential, this helps prevent heart problems as well as cancers.*

*Appetizers*

## <u>Orange Pecans</u>

1    cup sugar
½  cup water
1    tbsp. orange juice
1    orange rind, grated
2    cups pecan halves
Pinch of salt

      Mix sugar and water in saucepan.  Cook without stirring until it forms a soft ball.  Remove from heat and let stand 5 minutes.  Stir in orange rind and juice and salt.  Add pecans and stir mixture until sugar begins to crystallize.

*Karen's mother prepared this often for her family  and was usually made at Christmas time.  It is very easy to make and always enjoyed by the crowd.*

## Spinach Squares

2    pkgs frozen chopped spinach, thawed and squeezed dry
1    lb. shredded cheddar cheese
4    tsp. melted butter on cookie sheet
3    eggs
1    cup flour
1    cup milk
1    tsp. salt
1    tsp. baking powder

      Mix together eggs, flour, milk salt and baking powder and then mix in spinach and cheese.  Spread on cookie sheet.  Bake 35 minutes at 350 degrees.  Cool 10 minutes before cutting squares.

*Maggie has been making this recipe for many years.  This is a very good appetizer but can also be served with meals as a side dish. Tastings were very favorable.*

## Shrimp Spread

1   (3oz. ) pkg. cream cheese
1   cup sour cream
1   pkg. Good Seasons Italian Dressing Mix
2   tsp. lemon juice
1   can (4 1/2 oz.) shrimp

Blend and serve with crackers or chips.


*Party food with whimsy....prepares  quickly and the Italian Dressing gives it a good taste.  Very good served with Crostini.*

*To prepare Crostini, slice French baguettes ½ inch thick.  Brush olive oil on both sides and bake on cookie sheet for 20 minutes at 350 degrees.  Turn over after 10 minutes and bake other side.*

## Sausage Balls

1   lb. sausage
1   lb. sharp cheese (grated)
2   cups bisquick

Mix sausage and cheese together, then add bisquick. Make into small balls. Place on cookie sheet and bake at 350 degrees until brown. Makes 46-48 balls.

*Nancy has been preparing this dish for a long time and has never met anyone who did not enjoy. Our ladies think she should be "cook of the year". She makes a lot of dishes that are served at our get-togethers. This recipe can easily be doubled. They go fast!*

## Smoked Gouda-Chorizo Jalapeno Poppers

2 links Mexican chorizo, casings removed
1/2 lb. smoked Gouda, shredded
1/4 cup finely chopped red onions
1 egg
1/2 cup cream cheese
3 tbsp. sour cream
1 tbsp. hot sauce (recommended: Frank's Red Hot)
12 large jalapeno peppers, stemmed, seeded and halved
Salt and  pepper

  Preheat oven to 375 degrees F.   Brown chorizo in a skillet over medium-high heat, about 8 to 10 minutes.   Drain and place into a large mixing bowl. Add the cheese, red onion, egg, cream cheese, sour cream, hot sauce, and salt and pepper, to taste. Press into jalapeno halves and assemble on a parchment lined baking sheet. Bake until golden and bubbly, about 20 minutes.  You can substitute pork or turkey Italian sausage for chorizo.  If you have any mix left over, this makes a great stuffing for twice baked potato.


*Doris shares this favorite appetizer.  The ingredients make this dish good, good, good.*

*Fed by Grace*

## Spiced Nuts

1     cup sugar
½     tsp. cinnamon
1/3   cup evaporated milk
1     tsp. water
½     tsp. vanilla
1 ½  cup unsalted nuts

Mix in heavy 1 quart saucepan until well blended: sugar, cinnamon and evaporated milk.  Cook and stir over medium heat until mixture comes to a boil and sugar is dissolved.  Boil until candy reaches soft-ball stage (234°) stirring often.  Add water and vanilla; mix well.  Add nuts and stir well.  Spoon onto waxed paper in small pieces.

*This recipe is one of DeAnn's grandmothers.  She's enjoyed these during the Holiday season since girlhood.*

## Stuffed Strawberries

20  large fresh strawberries, divided
1   (3-oz) package cream cheese, softened
2   tbsp. finely chopped walnuts or pecans
1 ½ tbsp. powdered sugar
1   tsp. orange liqueur (optional)

      Make stuffing and prep strawberries a day ahead.  Fill strawberries no more than 4 hours before serving.
      Dice 2 strawberries, and set aside.  Cut a thin slice from stem end of each remaining strawberries, forming a base for strawberries to stand on.  Cut each strawberry into four wedges, starting at pointed ends and cutting to but not through stem ends.  Beat cream cheese at medium speed with an electric mixer until fluffy.  Stir in diced strawberries, walnuts, powdered sugar, and if desired, liqueur. Spoon or pipe about 1 teaspoon mixture into each strawberry.

*This recipe does take a little time to prepare but is a favorite among chefs.  It makes an appealing, colorful and tasty dish.  This is one you must try-- always a hit and will add some color to that buffet.*

*Fed by Grace*

## Sweet/Sour Kielbasa

2     lbs. kielbasa sausage
1     bottle prepared chili sauce
¾    cup red currant jelly
1     tsp. lemon juice
2     tsp. mustard
1     (20-ounce) can pineapple, chunks, drained

Slice kielbasa ¼" thick and cook over low heat for 10 minutes. Drain off excess fat and set aside.  In same skillet, stir in chili sauce, jelly, lemon juice and mustard.  Heat slowly, then add pineapple and kielbasa.  Simmer for 15 to 20 minutes before serving.

*This is an outstanding Low Country dish.  If you lose your partner at a party, check the crowd at the buffet table.  Sure you will find him eating kielbasa dipped in a delicious sauce.*

*Kielbasa is a catchall name for highly seasoned polish sausages and  traditionally made with pork.*

## Taco Dip

1   jar of favorite salsa
1   lb.  ground meat (chicken or turkey)
1   can  refried beans
1   pkg. taco seasoning
1   container sour cream
2   cups shredded cheese
1   bag tortilla chips
Green onion

     Prepare the ground meat by browning and then follow the instructions on the taco packet.  Layer the refried beans, the prepared meat, and the green onion.  Lay these over the sour cream, then add the cheese, then cover everything with the salsa.  Dip and enjoy.


*Tam's good friend, Bobbi, gave her this recipe.  It makes a good, filling party dish.  Also makes a hit with the family as a casserole served with a green salad.*

## Vidalia Onion Dip

2  tbsp.  butter or margarine
3  large Vidalia onions, coarsely chopped
2  cups (8 oz.) shredded Swiss cheese
2  cups mayonnaise
1  cup (8oz.) can sliced water chestnuts, drained and chopped
¼  cup dry white wine
1  garlic clove, minced
½  tsp.  hot sauce

Melt butter in a large skillet over medium-high heat. Add onion, and sauté 10 minutes or until tender. Stir together shredded Swiss cheese and next 5 ingredients. Stir in onion, blending well. Spoon mixture into a lightly greased 2-quart baking dish. Bake at 375 degrees for 25 minutes, and let stand 10 minutes. Serve with tortilla chips or cracker. Prep: 15 minutes, Bake: 25 minutes, Stand: 10 minutes.

*The Vidalia cooks are assured that the "Vidalia Onion" is the best and they are shipped all over the world. This recipe is one of their favorites and appears in many cookbooks.*

## Veggie Bars

| | |
|---|---|
| 2 | pkg. crescent rolls (8 pack) |
| ¾ | cup mayonnaise |
| 2 | pkg. cream cheese (8oz), softened |
| 1 | pkg. Hidden Valley Ranch Dressing Mix |
| 1 to 2 | cups finely chopped veggies (broccoli, carrots, cauliflower, green peppers, onions, mushrooms) |

Cover bottom of jelly roll pan with the rolls. Bake at 350° for 7-8 minutes. Cool. Mix together cream cheese, mayo and dressing mix. Spread mixture over cool rolls. Add veggies over the top of the mixture. Press down on veggies with wax paper to set. (I generally use broccoli, cauliflower & carrots.) Refrigerate for an hour or so before serving.

*This is a recipe given to DeAnn by a longtime family friend, Linda Morris. She thinks it deserves a special place among the appetizers. It is delicious for a buffet or can be served as a side dish.*

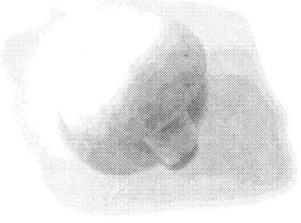

Fed by Grace

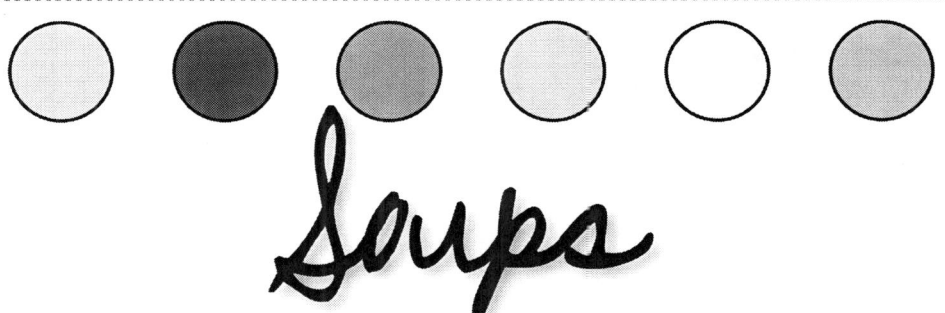

# Soups

Soup can be the beginning of a meal or a meal in itself with bread and salad. It is a good rescue for about –to-be discarded leftovers such as vegetables. In the earlier days, there was always a pot of soup simmering on the back burner of the stove for a long time to develop its full flavor. The South's claim to fame is the popular "Chicken and Dumplings", one of the main dishes that put Cracker Barrel on the map. Chowders are a favorite close to coastal areas and rivers where seafood and fish is easily accessible. Stews are usually made with more meat and sometimes is used as the main course. Soups and stews took longer to cook in earlier days, one had to be more creative with spices and flavors. In today's world, commercial aids would amaze our mothers and grandmothers.

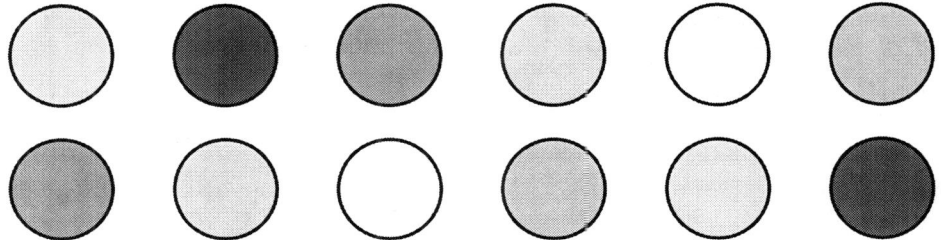

## Baked Potato Soup

```
4     large potatoes
2/3 cup butter or margarine
2/3 cup flour
6     cup milk
¾     tsp. salt
½     tsp. black pepper
4     green onions, chopped and divided
12    slices of bacon, fried, crumbled and divided
1 ¼  cups shredded cheddar cheese, divided
1     (8 ounce) carton sour cream
```

Bake potatoes, scoop our pulp. Melt butter in heavy saucepan over low heat. Add flour. Stir until smooth. Cook 1 minute stirring constantly. Gradually add all milk. Cook over medium heat, stirring constantly until thick and bubbly. Add potato pulp, salt, pepper, 2 tbsp. onion, ½ cup bacon and 1 cup cheese. Cook until heated. Stir in sour cream. Add extra milk if necessary, for desired thickness. Serve with remaining onion, bacon and cheese. Serves 10 cups.

*This recipe is shared with us by Mandy, wife of Pastor Jay Thompson. When we asked Jay for his favorite recipe, he said " I will get you one". He never came through but Mandy did. We have a feeling about who the cook is in this household.*

## Bean Soup

2   lbs Great Northern Beans
7   cups of water
1   cup of diced carrots
1   cup of diced onions
1   cup of diced celery
2   tbsp. of chopped dried parsley
Ham bone with meat
Salt and pepper to taste after cooking

Soak and rinse dried beans; combine all ingredients in slow cooker. Cover. Cook on high 5-6 hours or low 11-12 hours.

*Jim Oliver, outstanding cook in Hilton Head, shared this recipe with Maggie long ago. It is a very good way to cook Northern beans and it makes a good nourishing meal. Bake some good cornbread to go with it.*

## Broccoli Soup

½   cup diced green pepper
2     cups chopped frozen broccoli, cooked
¼   cup diced onion
1 ½ cups water
1     tbsp. butter
1     cup evaporated milk
½    tsp. curry powder
Salt and pepper to taste

    Puree first 4 ingredients in blender.  Pour into a large sauce pan and add remaining ingredients.  Heat and serve.  Serves 4.

*This is one of Nancy's stand-bys  and it is always enjoyed.*

## Brunswick Stew

1  large hen
1   pound small lima beans or butterbeans
2   pounds potatoes, slivered
1  pound white onions, sliced
1  large size can tomatoes or 2 fresh tomatoes
1  large size can corn or 6 fresh corn ears
½ pound butter
Salt, lemon juice, and pepper to taste

      Clean and cut up chicken, cook until tender and falling off bones.  Meanwhile cook butterbeans, onions, and potatoes in very little water until well done.  Add these vegetables to the chicken.  Also add butter (unless the chicken is very fat), corn, tomatoes, and season to taste with salt, pepper and lemon juice.  Cook  very slowly, stirring often until very thick.  Add hot pepper to taste if desired.

*From Nettie Thomas, a neighbor and friend of Nancy.  Everyone in the South has to have a favorite Brunswick stew.  Maybe this one will become that for you.*

> *The more you eat, the less flavor.*
> *The less you eat, the more flavor.*

## Chicken 'N Squash Soup

| | |
|---|---|
| 1 | broiler chicken (4 pounds) cut up |
| 13 | cups water |
| 5 | lb. butternut squash, peeled and cubed |
| 1 ¼ | lb. fresh kale, chopped |
| 6 | med. carrots, chopped |
| 2 | large onions, chopped |
| 3 | tsp. salt. |

Place chicken and water in large pan. Bring to a boil and reduce heat. Cover and simmer for 1 hour or until chicken is done. Remove chicken from broth. Stain the broth and skim away fat. Return broth to pan. Add the squash, kale, carrots and onions. Bring to boil. Reduce heat, cover and simmer for 25-30 minutes or until the veggies are tender. When chicken is cooked enough to handle, remove meat from bones and cut into bite-size pieces. Discard bones and skin. Add chicken and salt to taste. Heat for serving.

*We certainly wanted to share this First prize soup winner from Taste of Home Magazine 2008. It is delicious and it has some interesting ingredients.*

## Chicken Noodle Soup

2     cups water
1     (32-ounce ) carton fat-free, less-sodium chicken broth
1     tbsp. olive oil
½    cup pre-chopped onion
½    cup pre-chopped celery
½    tsp. freshly ground black pepper
1     med.  carrot, chopped
6     oz.  fusilli pasta (wide egg noodles, rotini, or orzo)
2 ½ cups shredded skinless, boneless rotisserie chicken breast
2     tbsp. chopped fresh flat-leaf parsley

      Combine 2 cups water and chicken broth in a microwave-safe dish, and microwave on HIGH for 5 minutes.  While broth mixture heats, place a large saucepan over medium-high heat with oil added to pan.  Swirl to coat.  Add onion, celery, salt, pepper, and carrot.  Sauté 3 minutes or until almost tender, stirring frequently.  Add hot broth mixture and pasta.  Bring to boil.  Cook 7 minutes or until pasta is almost al dente.  Stir in chicken.  Cook until thoroughly heated.  Stir in parsley.

*Here is a true Southerner's comfort food for every member of the family.  This can be just the dish you may need to pamper the young ones when they are under the weather.*

## Clam Chowder

½   pound bacon, diced
3   (6 ½ oz.) cans minced clams, juice reserved
2   medium onions
3   cups diced potatoes
2   cups sliced baby carrots
½   cup butter
1   lb. Velveeta cheese
½   tsp. garlic powder
1   cup milk
Salt to taste

In large pot, cook bacon until crisp. Pour off grease. Add juice from clams. Add onions, carrots, potatoes, and butter. Cover and cook about 15 minutes until vegetables are tender. Add cheese, garlic powder and stir until soup comes to a simmer. Add clams, then enough milk to bring the mixture to consistency of a thick soup. Season lightly to taste (liquid from seafood is salty). Do not over-cook clams.

*This soup is very hearty and most men love it. This makes a good meal served with toasted French bread and a green salad.*

Titus 2

## French Onion Soup with Croutons

3      lb. peeled onions , sliced thick
½      cup butter
¾      cup flour
1 ½ tsp. pepper
2      tbsp. paprika
1      bay leaf
1      cup white wine
3      qt. beef bouillon
       croutons
6      English muffins
12     slices mozzarella cheese
Salt as needed

Sauté onions in butter until soft.  Make a paste with flour and small amounts of warm liquid from sautéed onions.  Add paste and next 5  ingredients.  Simmer 10 minutes.  Add bouillon.  Cover and simmer 2 hours.  Refrigerate overnight.  Preheat to serve.  Split English muffins into halves, cut into quarters and put on top of soup. Lay Mozzarella slices on top and melt.

*This French onion soup is very easy to prepare according to Nancy. It is especially good when cooked with Vidalia or Glennville onions.*

## Fresh Berry Soup

| | |
|---|---|
| 1 | qt. fresh orange juice |
| 1 1/3 | cup yogurt |
| 1 1/3 | cup buttermilk |
| 1 1/3 | cup sour cream |
| 1 | tbsp. honey (more to taste) |
| 1 | tbsp. fresh lemon or lime juice |
| | dash of cinnamon |
| | dash of nutmeg |
| 1 ½ | pint fresh berries (raspberries, blackberries or strawberries) |

Whisk together juice, yogurt, buttermilk, sour cream, honey, lemon (or lime) juice, cinnamon and nutmeg. Chill thoroughly. Wash and drain the berries left whole. Large strawberries should be cut in halves.

*The ingredients in this soup will make anything good. This is a refreshing change for a hot summer day's lunch along with a chicken salad sandwich-- yum, yum, good.*

*Adding berries to your diet will help fight the signs of aging, provide energy, and aid in preventing certain diseases. Raspberries boast a healthy dose of ellagic acid, a powerful cancer-fighting substance and also fiber.*

## Ginger-Carrot Soup

```
2    tbsp. cooking oil
3    cups thinly sliced onion
2    tbsp. sugar
1/8  tsp. freshly ground black pepper
2    tbsp. grated fresh ginger
8    carrots
1    sweet potato
6    cups chicken broth
1    cup half and half or light cream
```

In large skillet heat oil over medium heat and add sliced onions, sugar, and pepper.  Reduce heat to low.  Cover and cook 30 minutes, stirring  twice.  Add ginger.  Cook uncovered 20 to 30 minutes more or until onion is golden brown, stirring occasionally.  Divide in half and set aside.  Peel carrots and sweet potato, and cut in 1-inch pieces.  In large saucepan combine broth, carrots, and sweet potato.  Bring to boiling and reduce heat.  Simmer, covered for 40 minutes or until vegetables are very tender.  Add half the onions and puree until nearly smooth in blender or 2 cups at a time in food processor.  Add cream and heat through.  Season to taste with salt and freshly ground black pepper.

*Here is another award winning soup by the "soup queen" Nancy. They just keep getting better and better.*

## Hearty Potato Soup

6    potatoes, peeled and cut into ½ inch cubes
2    med. onions diced
2    celery ribs, thinly sliced
2    (14 ½ oz.) cans low sodium fat-free chicken broth
1    tsp. dried basil
1    tsp. salt
1    tsp. pepper

      Combine these ingredients in a 4 ½ qt. pot or slow cooker. In slow cooker, cover and cook on high for 3 hours or until veggies are tender. To cook in pot on top of stove, cook ½ hour to ¾ hour until veggies are tender. Mix together 2 tbsp. flour into 1 cup half and half and then stir into veggies. Blend and heat thoroughly. Serve in Italian bread bowls and garnish if desired. Yields 8 ½ cups.

*Nancy says this is an awesome, comfort, southern, soul potato soup. Super easy, super quick and super good.*

## **Manhattan Clam Chowder**

1/4    lb, bacon  (diced and fried)
1       large onion (diced)
2       carrots (diced)
3       ribs of celery (diced)
1       tbsp . dried parsley flakes
1       lb. (12 oz)  can of tomatoes
2       8-oz cans of clams with liquid
3       med. potatoes (cubed)
1 1/2 tsp. dried crushed thyme
Salt and pepper to taste

      Combine all ingredients in slow cooker.  Cover.  Cook on low 8-10 hours.


*This is another recipe given to Maggie long ago by a dear friend who grew up on the Maryland shore.  This recipe has proved to be very good and tasty.*

Soups

## Oyster Stew

1    pint oysters, washed and drained
¼  cup butter or margarine
1    quart milk
1    tsp. lemon juice
Salt and pepper to taste
Garlic powder—dash

      In saucepan put butter and seasonings, using medium heat. After butter melted, add oysters and cook until edges curl.  Add milk and let heat until hot through, but do not boil as milk will curdle. Serve with oysterettes or saltines.

*For the Oyster Stew lovers, this recipe especially good and easy to prepare.  A favorite to serve on a cold winter night.*

## Pam's Vegetable Soup

2   cans VegAll
1   can corn
1   green beans,  French cut
1   large can crushed tomatoes
1   lb.  ground beef

     Brown ground beef. Drain and add to vegetables. Heat soup on low to medium  heat for 1 hour.  Salt and pepper to taste.  Serves 8.


     Optional:
1  can Rotel for a little spice
1  can of sliced okra for gumbo feel
1  bay leaf


*Pam Wells, wife of our Minister of Music, Michael, shares one of her easy soup recipes.  This is a really quick-to-make version, plus some simple variations.  Here you have a perfect dish to serve on those days (too many of them) when your family is so busy and on different schedules.*

## Scotch Broth Soup

2    lbs. good beef shank or stew beef
3    qt. Water
2    cups fresh or frozen peas
2    small or 1 cup turnips or rutabaga (root ball)
1    cup diced cabbage
1    large onion, chopped
2    carrots, grated
½    cup pearl barley
1    tbsp. fresh parsley, chopped
Salt and pepper to taste

      Simmer the beef 3 hours in 3 qts. water. Remove the beef from the stock. Add to the stock all the chopped vegetables and the seasonings and simmer for 1 ½ hours. Serves 6.

*This is a Scottish recipe from Nancy's Mom who was born in Scotland. As a result this one has always been a real family favorite.*

## Spicy Pumpkin or Butternut Squash Soup

2      tbsp. olive oil
1      Vidalia onion (chopped)
2      stalks celery (chopped)
3      cloves  garlic minced
1      tbsp. curry powder
         Sauté the above and set aside
6      cups chicken broth stock
 1 1/4 cups pumpkin or butternut squash, peeled and cut up
1      plantain (large green banana), chopped and diced
1      tbsp. red sage
1      tbsp. oregano
Pinch salt and pepper
½ tsp. hot pepper sauce

*Mix in a large pot and simmer together for 20 minutes.  Add salt and pepper to taste.  Add ½ tsp. hot pepper sauce.  Add sautéed  ingredients to soup and cook for 20 additional minutes. Put a small amount at a time in the blender or food processor and blend until smooth and creamy.*

*Chives*
*Pumpkin seeds ( roasted 5 minutes @ 350 degrees)*
*Garnish with chives and roasted pumpkin seeds.  Allow to cool.*

*Nancy gives us another wonderful soup recipe.  It's different and delicious.*

# Tucson Vegetable Soup with Sage

3    tbsp. olive oil  4 cloves diced garlic
4    tbsp. chopped fresh sage leaves  1 medium onion
1    cup fresh or frozen peas
1    cup ½ inch pieces green beans
1    cup diced zucchini
1    cup diced carrots
½    cup diced celery
1    peeled and diced sweet potato
1    16 oz. can white beans (or black beans), rinsed and drained
6    cups reduced sodium chicken broth
½    tsp. crushed red pepper flakes
¼    cup low fat ricotta cheese
Salt and pepper to taste
Cooked white or rosette rice

Heat oil, sauté sage, garlic, onions for 5 minutes.  Add peas, green beans, zucchini, carrots, and celery, potato, white beans and stir over medium heat 3 to 5 minutes.  Add broth and red pepper flakes,.  Simmer until veggies are tender for 15 to 20 minutes.  Season with salt and pepper.  Top each serving with ricotta cheese if desired.  Very good served with rice.

*Bob, Nancy's better half, wanted us to share this one with all of you.  This happens to be his very favorite.*

> *Soup is the perfect one-dish meal---it contains all the food groups, and reheats well on those days when everyone is busy.*

## Turkey Tortilla Soup

3   6-inch corn tortillas, cut in strips
2   tbsp. cooking oil
1   cup purchased red or green salsa
2   14oz. cans reduced sodium chicken broth
2   cups cubed cooked turkey (12 ounces)
1   large zucchini, coarsely chopped (lime wedges optional)
Sour cream and cilantro (optional)

In a large skillet cook tortilla strips in hot oil until crisp.  Remove with slotted spoon and drain on paper towels.

In a large sauce pan combine salsa and chicken broth and bring to a boil over medium heat.  Stir in turkey and zucchini, and heat.  Serve in bowls, top with tortilla strips, lime wedges, sour cream and cilantro.  Makes 4 servings.

*Audrey promises this is a rib-sticking and no fuss meal for a busy night which takes 20 minutes from start to finish.*

## Vegetable Soup, Italian Style

1    pkg. (12 oz.) uncooked small pasta shells or corkscrew pasta
2    cloves garlic, minced
1    bay leaf
2    tsp. Italian seasoning blend
1    can (28 ounces) crushed tomatoes in puree
1    tsp. salt
2    cups water
½   tsp. white pepper
1    can (1.5 oz.) white beans, rinsed and drained
1    bag (16 oz.) frozen vegetable medley, such as broccoli, green
beans, carrots
1    can (14 ½ oz.) vegetable broth
1    can (12oz.) coca-cola
Juice of ½ lemon

      Cook pasta according to package directions, drain, and set
aside.  Combine tomatoes, water, beans, broth, coca-cola, garlic and
bay leaf in large Dutch oven.  Add seasoning blend, salt and white
pepper.  Mix well. Bring to a boil over high heat.  Reduce heat to low
and simmer 10 to 15 minutes, stirring occasionally.  Add frozen
vegetables to Dutch oven and return to a boil over high heat.  Stir in
pasta and reduce heat to low. Simmer 10 to 15 minutes or until
heated through.  Remove bay leaf.  Stir in lemon juice.  Ladle soup
into bowls.  Garnish, if desired.  Serve immediately.  Makes 6 to 8
servings.

*Amy and her family enjoy this soup because it is a meal within it-
self.  Some mighty good  ingredients for some good eating.*

 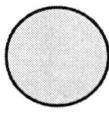 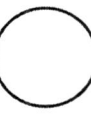   

# Salads

Salads are a healthy part of today's diets and had a prominent place in many of the older cookbooks. In earlier days, salads were made with root vegetables such as fresh grown, cabbage and kale which were sometimes kept in cellars. Chicken salad has always been the most popular meat salad category for it played an important part in home entertaining and of course everyone eats chicken, one way or another. Potato Salad was one of the mainstays on a picnic menu along with fried chicken. It is still very popular in today's world. In earlier days, home grown tomatoes were plentiful and served many different ways such as sliced or mixed with other green and raw vegetables. Today's salads range from fresh greens or congealed fruits to meats and seafood. In earlier days, dressings were made from scratch. Then as now, a good rule of Thumb is the old-time advice "have a spendthrift for oil, a miser for vinegar, a wise man for salt and a madcap to stir the ingredients up and mix together. Cooks of yesterday used mayonnaise dressing for some vegetables and French dressing for lettuce. Now, the blender is used for a quick tasty dressing of many kinds.

*Fed by Grace*

## Almond Chicken Salad

4     cups cubed cooked chicken
1 ½ cup seedless grapes
1     cup chopped celery
2/3 cup slice green onions
3     hard-cooked eggs, chopped
½   cup mayonnaise
¼   cup sour cream
1     tbsp. Prepared mustard
1     tsp. salt
½   tsp. pepper
¼   tsp. onion powder
¼   tsp. celery salt
1/8 tsp. paprika
½   cup slivered almonds, toasted

   In a large bowl, combine chicken, grapes, celery, onions and eggs.  In another bowl, combine mayonnaise, sour cream, prepared mustard, salt, pepper, onion powder, celery salt, dry mustard, and paprika.  Stir until smooth.  Pour over the chicken mixture and toss gently.  Stir in almonds and serve immediately, or refrigerate and add the almonds just before serving.

*Everyone's favorite recipe file should include a good chicken salad and this one proved to be one of the best.  It will be a hit at a luncheon, bridal shower, etc.  Serve with a yummy croissant.*

*Sometimes when in a hurry, you can use a store-bought dressing. If so, put a clove of garlic in the dressing to give it some zip.*

## **Bing Cherry Congealed Salad**

1   16.5 ounce can pitted Bing cherries, drained, juice reserved
1   15 ounce) can crushed pineapple, drained with juice reserved
1   6 ounce) package cherry gelatin
1   3 ounce) package cream cheese
6   fluid ounces coke-cola
1   cup chopped pecans

In a sauce pan, combine reserved cherry juice and pineapple juice to equal 1 cup. Bring to boil, add gelatin and whisk together. Remove heat and add cream cheese and blend together until smooth. Add cola and heat until mixture becomes fluffy. Fold in cherries, pineapple, and nuts. Pour into molded container. Chill 6 to 8 hours or until firm.

*This salad is easy to make, delicious and shows well on a buffet. It is a nice fall dish that will blend in with the season.*

## Broccoli Salad

2      cup miracle whip
¼      cup sugar
¼      cup  red wine vinegar
2       bags broccoli  (1lb bag of florets or 2 bunches, broken up)
½      cup purple onion, chopped
1      cup golden raisins
1      cup cashews
1      lb. bacon, cooked and crumbled

  Combine all ingredients and chill before serving.


*Amy gives us another broccoli salad.  You have been given a few to try and compare.  Different ingredients  make these salads more appetizing.  Enjoy all of them.*

## Broccoli Slaw Salad

1    16 oz.  broccoli slaw mix
2    pkg.  ramen beef  noodles (with seasoning packet)
2    bunches green onion, sliced
1    cup sunflower seeds
1    cup toasted slivered almonds
      DRESSING:  Mix 1 cup oil,  ½ cup sugar,  ½ cup white or rice
      vinegar.
pkg. of seasoning from  noodles

      Mix broccoli mix, beef noodles and onions together.  Add
dressing.  Chill for 2 hours Before serving add seeds and toasted almonds.


*Tam likes this dish because it is a good substitute for cabbage slaw
and very tasty with the noodles.*

*No two Christians will ever meet for the last time.*

## Carol's Broccoli Salad

4    cups cut up broccoli
¼   cup raisins or dried cranberries
¼   cup pecans, chopped
8    slices bacon , cooked crispy and crumbled
¼   cup chopped green onions
     Dressing: 1 Cup mayonnaise, ¼ cup sugar, 2 tbsp. wine vinegar

      Toss broccoli, raisins, nuts, bacon and onions in a large bowl.
Add dressing and toss well.


*This recipe is from Carol, sister-in-law of Nancy, and everyone
loves this salad.   We have it often at our Titus 2 get-together.*

## Celebration Tossed Salad

| | |
|---|---|
| 1 | large  bag romaine lettuce |
| 1 | carton grape tomatoes |
| 1 | large ripe avocado, sliced |
| 3 | oz. blue cheese, crumbled |
| 1 | med.  red or sweet onion, sliced |
| 6 | slices cooked bacon, crumbled |

Place lettuce in bottom of large salad bowl.  Arrange vegetables on top of lettuce.  Sprinkle blue cheese and bacon over all. When ready to serve, toss with dressing.  Dressing: ¾ cup vegetable oil, 1 tsp. salt, ¼ cup vinegar, 4 tsps. Sugar, 1 clove minced garlic, pepper to taste.  Combine all ingredients in jar and shake well.

*Outstanding salad which is easy to prepare and very satisfying to the palate.  Be sure to serve it when you are having a celebration meal.*

*To make lettuce more crisp, wash and drain, then roll gently in a towel and refrigerate before using.*

## Church Salad

1  lg. pkg. cherry Jello
2  cups hot water (boiling)
1  can cherry pie filling
1  lg. can crushed pineapple
       Mix and let congeal
Topping: 1 (8oz.) sour cream,  1 (8oz.) cream cheese, and ½ cup
sugar

       Cream all together and spread on salad and then sprinkle
with nuts.


*Karen  shares  her mother's favorite recipe that she took to those
church pot luck dinners.  She always got special attention for her
cooking talents.*


## Congealed Cranberry Salad

2      small packages orange jello
1      can cranberry sauce or whole berry
1      lg. can crushed pineapple
1      can mandarin oranges, crushed
1      cup chopped pecans

       Dissolve jello in 2 cups hot water.  Add remaining ingredients.
Mix and chill until set.


*This is such an easy salad to make, tasty and especially festive for
the holidays. It is very good when served with ham or turkey.*

## Cranberry-Walnut Cabbage Slaw

5     cups shredded cabbage
1     carrot, shredded
¼     cup finely chopped celery
¼     chopped onion
1/3   cup pecans, toasted
¼     cup dried cranberries
Dressing
2     tbsp. olive oil
2     tbsp. balsamic vinegar
1     tsp. brown sugar
1     tbsp. soy sauce

Combine dressing ingredients in large mixing bowl. Combine cabbage, all vegetables, nuts and cranberries. Add dressing. Toss to coat and chill in covered bowl. Makes 10 servings.

*This recipe gives slaw a lot of character and the dressing hits the spot.*

*Hollow out center of head of cabbage. Turn outer leaves out to curl like a flower. Fill with slaw, dips, fresh fruits and other salads. Makes a pretty presentation on your table.*

## Grape Salad

3  pounds red grapes
8  oz. cream cheese
8  oz. sour cream
½ cup sugar
1  cup chopped pecans

Mix together and stir in grapes.

*This is an unusual way to use grapes but it creates an enjoyable salad. This would be a good one to serve at a bridge luncheon and would fit in well with other salads on a buffet.*

## Congealed Lime-Lemon Salad

1     8oz. box lime gelatin
1     8oz. box lemon gelatin
2     cups boiling water
1     8oz. pkg. cream cheese
½    cup mayonnaise
1     can condensed milk
1     2oz.can crushed pineapple
1     cup chopped pecans

     Let cream cheese soften to room temperature; beat until smooth; add mayonnaise and condensed milk; mix well and set aside. Dissolve gelatins in boiling water; add gelatin and remaining ingredients to cheese mixture; blend together and pour into mold. Chill to set.

*Congealed salads are always a hit on a luncheon buffet. You should make this recipe a day before serving. The color of this salad will add that decorative flair to your dining table. It is easy, elegant, and enjoyable.*

## Doris's Broccoli Salad

| | |
|---|---|
| 1 | head broccoli |
| 5 | slices cooked bacon, crumbled |
| 1/2 | cup chopped red onion |
| 1/2 | cup raisins, optional |
| 8 | oz. sharp Cheddar, cut into very small chunks |
| 1 | cup mayonnaise |
| 2 | tbsp. white vinegar |
| ¼ | cup sugar |
| 1/2 | cup halved cherry tomatoes |

Salt and freshly ground black pepper

Trim off the large leaves from the broccoli stem. Remove the tough stalk at the end and wash broccoli head thoroughly. Cut the head into flowerets and the stem into bite-size pieces. Place in a large bowl. Add the crumbled bacon, onion, raisins if using, and cheese. In a small bowl, combine the remaining ingredients, stirring well. Add to broccoli mixture and toss gently.(If desired, broccoli could be blanched to get rid of the raw taste. Just make sure all the water is out of the broccoli if you blanch it). You may also add chopped almonds or pecans. Pancetta could be substituted for the bacon. Serves 6 to 8 servings

*This makes a great side dish for chicken or fish. Doris says it is a hit every time she makes it.*

# Mediterranean Tuna and White Bean Salad

2    (6 oz.) cans chunk light tuna in water
1    (15 oz.) can cannellini beans or white kidney beans
1    small red onion, diced
3    tbsp. capers
½    cup fresh parsley, chopped
Dressing:
       2 tbsp extra virgin olive oil
       2 tbsp red wine vinegar
       2 tbsp freshly lemon juice
       1 tbsp dried oregano
       Salt and pepper to taste

Place the tuna in a large bowl and break apart the chunks with a fork.  Drain and rinse the cannellini beans and add to the bowl.  Add the diced red onion, capers, slivered sun-dried tomatoes and chopped pepper.  Mix well to combine.  In a small bowl, whisk together the olive oil, red wine vinegar, lemon juice, oregano, salt and pepper.  Pour over the salad and mix well to combine.  Taste and adjust for seasonings.  For a main entrée, serve on a bed of chopped romaine lettuce.  Serves four.

*Karen finds this tasty salad to be a hurry-up dinner after that hectic day at work or shopping.*

## Napa Cabbage Salad

1     head Napa Cabbage
      blue cheese to taste
Dressing Ingredients:
1     large onion
1     tsp. salt
1/2  cup sugar (or to taste)
1     tsp. celery seed
½   cup white vinegar
1     cup peanut oil

      Blend all ingredients for dressing in food processer and let stand for 1 hour.  Slice and chop cabbage and arrange in salad bowl. Crumble blue cheese  (to taste) over cabbage.  Drizzle with dressing and serve.

*Maggie likes to serve this salad at a dinner party.   There are not too many recipes that call for Napa cabbage.  The dressing is the secret.*

## Orange Congealed Salad

3    oz. orange jello ( may also use peach, lime or strawberry)
½   cup water
1    small crushed pineapple
8    oz. cream cheese
8    oz. cool Whip
1    cup nuts

Bring water and pineapple to boil and then add jello. Remove and add cream cheese, then add cool whip and nuts. Refrigerate until set before serving.

*This is a favorite with Maggie and her family. It could almost make a good dessert. All flavors of jello are good used in this recipe.*

## Oriental Noodle Salad

2    packages baked Ramen Noodle soup Mix
½   cup slivered almonds
2    tbsp sesame seeds
1    tbsp canola oil
½   small green cabbage, shredded (about 4 cups)
1    bunch scallion or green onions,  chopped
2    medium carrots, shredded
     Dressing: ¼ cup orange juice, ¼ cup white cider vinegar, 2 tbsp. sugar, 2 tbsp. soy sauce, 1 tsp. sesame oil.

        Preheat oven to 350 degrees.  Crumble Ramen noodles onto a large baking sheet.  Add almonds, sesame seeds and canola oil.  Toss and bake for 5 minutes or until noodles are golden brown.  Let cool on baking sheet.  Prepare above salad dressing in a small bowl or jar with tight fitting lid.  Whisk or shake until the sugar has dissolved.  Refrigerate to store.  Shake prior to using.  Just before serving combine the cabbage, carrots and scallions in a large bowl. Add the toasted noodle mixture and the dressing.

Note: You can omit the carrots and scallion and substitute Mandarin Oranges.  By not fixing 4 cups, you can store the remaining dressing and put the noodle mixture in a baggy and save it for the next salad as well.

*Karen and her family enjoy this salad.  The different ingredients make it unusually good and appealing.*

## Potato Salad

| | |
|---|---|
| 1 | cup mayonnaise |
| 2 | t. vinegar |
| 1 | tsp. sugar |
| 1 ½ | tsp salt |
| 1 | tsp. pepper (or less) |
| 4 | cups (5-6 medium) cooked potatoes, cubed |
| 1 | cup sliced celery |
| 1 | cup chopped onion |
| 2 | hard-boiled eggs |

Combine mayonnaise, vinegar, sugar, salt, and pepper and stir in potatoes, celery, onion, and eggs. Cover and chill. Makes 5 servings.

*This is one of the old standbys. Our grandmothers and mothers always had a bowl of potato salad on the Sunday dinner table. It is always good and easy to make. Another 'Southern Tradition".*

> If you are not as close to God as you used to be, who moved?

## Seven Layer Salad

1      head lettuce, shredded
1      cup chopped celery
1      cup green pepper, chopped
1      med. Onion
1      box frozen petite green peas
1      lb. bacon, fried and crumbled
5      hard-boiled eggs, sliced
2      cups mayonnaise
2      tbsp sugar
3      cups shredded cheddar cheese

Using a pyrex dish, place a bed of chopped lettuce on the bottom; then, layer celery, onions, green peppers, green peas, and sliced boiled eggs. Then repeat this procedure for another layer. The order is really not that important, and they will not really constitute a solid layer. Mix mayonnaise and sugar together and spread on top. Sprinkle bacon and cheddar cheese on top of the entire dish. Cover tightly and leave overnight in refrigerator, allowing mayonnaise to permeate the whole thing.

*Maggie has given this recipe the title "Cousin Salad". It was given by one of her cousins who got it from her cousin, who got it from her cousin...get the idea. Every reunion ended up with several as every cousin brought one.*

> To keep cheese fresh, wrap with
> towel soaked in vinegar.

## Shrimp Salad

4     cups chopped cooked shrimp
¾    cup mayonnaise
4     thinly sliced green onions
2     diced celery ribs
2     tsp grated lemon rind
Salt to taste

Mix together, cover and put in refrigerator to flavor.

*No buffet or dinner party in Hilton Head was complete without a serving of shrimp salad or shrimp cocktail. This dish is delightful to serve with a croissant and fresh fruit for a luncheon.*

*1 pound of raw shrimp equals 2 cups cooked, peeled shrimp.*

## Southern Potato Salad

6    med. baking potatoes
3    eggs, boiled
3    tbsp mayonnaise
2    tbsp Durkee sauce
½ cup sour cream
2    tsp  oil and vinegar dressing
½ tsp  Dijon mustard
½ cup minced onion
Salt and pepper to taste
Fresh parsley

Cook unpeeled potatoes in salted water until tender.  While potatoes are cooking mash hard boiled eggs in a bowl.  Combine mayonnaise, Durkee sauce, sour cream, dressing, mustard and onion.  Add salt and pepper.  When warm, mix with eggs and dressing.  Adjust salt and pepper.  When serving, decorate with parsley.
Yield: 12 servings.

*This is another one of those favorites from the Plantation Cooks in Albany, Ga.  Potato salad was prepared for every meal  on the plantations.  Southern staple.*

# Salads

## Spinach Salad

| | |
|---|---|
| ½ | cup vegetable oil |
| 1 | tsp. salt |
| ¼ | cup cider vinegar |
| ½ | tsp. pepper |
| 2 | tbsp. sugar |
| 6 | strips cooked bacon, crumbled |
| 1 | tbsp. Worcestershire sauce |
| 1 | minced clove garlic |
| 2 | hard-boiled eggs, chopped |
| ½ | cup ketchup |
| 1 | red or sweet onion, sliced |

Spinach (bagged or fresh)

Combine oil, vinegar, sugar, Worcestershire sauce, garlic, ketchup, salt and pepper in a jar and shake well. Refrigerate. Layer spinach, bacon, eggs and onion in bowl and toss with dressing.

*This is very simple to make and can be a family favorite. Remember to eat your spinach, it will make you strong.*

## Summer Strawberry Salad

6  cups chopped romaine lettuce
3  cups sliced fresh strawberries
2  cups cubed fresh pineapple
1  banana, sliced
¼  cup water
¼  cup cream of coconut
2  tbsp. lemon juice
1  tbsp. yellow mustard
½  tsp. ground ginger
¼  cup sliced almonds, toasted

In a 4-quart bowl toss together romaine, strawberries, pineapple, and banana. Salad may be assembled and refrigerated—nightly covered—up to 1 hour ahead. For dressing, in a small bowl whisk together water, cream of coconut, lemon juice, mustard, and ginger. Cover and refrigerate the dressing. To serve, toss greens and fruit mixture with dressing to coat. Sprinkle with almonds.

*Making this salad will satisfy that artistic talent that lives in the soul of every chef. The fresh fruit gives it a beautiful palette .*

*Lemon juice prevents discoloration of cut pieces of fresh fruits, avocado and mushrooms.*

## Ten Cup Salad

1    large can pineapple chunks, drained
1    large can mandarin oranges, drained
8    tbsp. coconut
1    tsp. coconut flavoring
2    cups grapes, cut in half
2    cups mini marshmallows
2    cups fat free sour cream
3    packets Splenda

      Combine all.  Keep refrigerated.

*This is a Weight Watcher recipe, with 1 cup equal to 3 points.  How delicious can it get!*

## Watergate Salad

1   large pkg. pistachio instant pudding mix
1   large can crushed pineapple, drained
½  cup miniature marshmallows
16  oz. Cool Whip
1   cup chopped pecans
1   cup coconut

Mix pudding mix and Cool Whip.  Fold in other ingredients. Chill before serving.

*Everyone loves this salad and the recipe has been around for a long time.  It's still a popular salad served at most buffet restaurants.*

# Wilted Lettuce Salad

1 head of lettuce
5-6 slices bacon
¼ cup red wine vinegar
½ cup sugar
1 tbsp. lemon juice
Salt and pepper

One head of lettuce torn into bite-size pieces. Fry bacon and set aside to crumble. To the hot bacon drippings, add the vinegar, lemon juice, sugar, salt and pepper. Stir over medium heat until hot and then pour over lettuce. Sprinkle bacon on top.

*This recipe has been a long time favorite of Maggie's family. It was given to her in the 70's by the chef at Bennie's Red Barn in St. Simons Island, Ga. This is the only salad they ever serve, and it became a favorite of many tourists from all over the world.*

# Breads

"Truly, bread is the staff of life" as well as being an art. Southern life could not be sustained without homemade breads. The better bread that you could make, the better cook you were. Bread making was considered a skill for any good cook. The smell of breads in the morning started our day off on the right track. Coming home from school in the afternoon and finding biscuits in the bread box was truly a treat. Some folk were known to make a hole in the middle of the biscuit and fill it with syrup. Old time kitchens always offered old-time homemade breads.

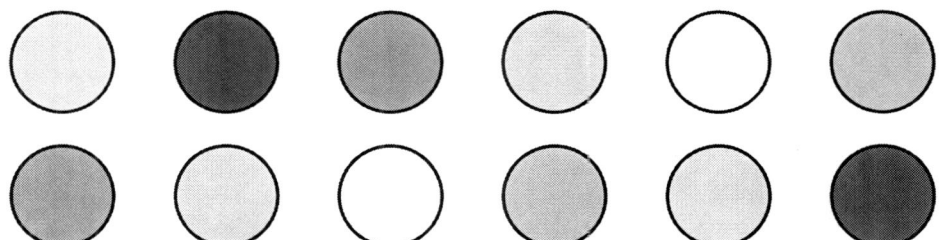

## Blueberry Muffins

| | |
|---|---|
| 1 | egg |
| ½ | cup milk |
| ¼ | cup oil |
| 1 ½ | cup flour |
| ½ | cup sugar |
| 1 | cup blueberries |

  Preheat oven to 400°.  Mix all ingredients and spoon into greased muffin tins.  Bake for about 20 minutes.

*DeAnn says that these muffins are absolutely delicious.  The secret is "not mixing" the batter too much.  Quick, easy and very good for you.  Enjoyed by the young and the old.*

## Broccoli Cornbread

1   box chopped broccoli, thawed and drained
1   stick melted butter
6   oz. cottage cheese
1   cup chopped onion
1   box Jiffy Corn Muffin Mix
1   tsp. salt
4   eggs

   Mix together and bake in a greased pan at 350 degrees for 40-45 minutes.

*Karen and her family enjoys this dish along with a good bowl of soup.*

*Broccoli is jam-packed with vitamins and minerals. It is a great cancer fighter. Eat it every chance you get.*

## Mexican Cornbread

1     diced onion
2     chopped banana peppers
1/3  cup Wesson oil
2     eggs, beaten
1     cup diced cheddar cheese
1     cup cream style corn
1     cup corn meal

Mix all together and bake in a greased pan at 375 degrees for 25 to 30 minutes or until brown.

*Karen claims this is a very good, home style cornbread. It is moist and delicious with plenty of corn and cheese.*

## Cheddar and Scallion Bread

8   oz.  sharp cheddar cheese, shredded or coarsely grated
6   oz. butter, at room temperature
4   scallions, finely chopped
2   cloves garlic, chopped
1   lb.  loaf ciabatta bread, cut in half horizontally
      kosher salt and freshly ground black pepper

      Place an oven rack in the center of the oven. Preheat the oven to 400 degrees F.  In a food processor, combine the cheese and butter.  Process until the mixture is smooth. Add the scallions and pulse until combined. Season with salt and pepper to taste. Spread the cheese mixture on the cut sides of the bread. Place on a baking sheet and bake for 10 to 12 minutes until golden.  Using a serrated knife, cut the bread into 1-inch thick slices and serve.

*Doris says this is a must to be served with the white bean and chicken chili recipe (see recipe in Entrees).*

*Ciabatta means "slipper" which leads many people to call the bread "slipper bread".  This bread was invented by Italian bakers and has become very popular throughout the rest of the world.*

## Chocolate Italian Biscotti

1       cup hazelnuts (or better, use pecans)
3       cups all purpose flour
1 ½   tsp. baking powder
1/8   tsp. salt
½       cup softened butter
1       cup sugar
5       oz. unsweetened chocolate
3       medium eggs (room temp)
1       tsp. vanilla extract

Roast nuts in oven at 350 degrees for 10 minutes. Reduce heat to 325 degrees. If using hazelnuts while warm rub between kitchen towel to remove skin. Coarsely chop the nuts and set aside. Microwave the chocolate in a glass bowl on medium for 2-3 minutes. Mix together the flour, baking powder, salt and set aside. In a large bowl with electric mixer beat together the butter and sugar. Add the eggs, 1 at a time. Add vanilla. Then add the melted and cooled chocolate. Add the dry ingredients and continue mixing until well blended. Fold in nuts on a lightly floured board and divide the dough in half and form 2 loaves about 14 inches long and 2 inches wide. Place on a greased cookie sheet. Bake at 325 degrees for 30 minutes. Allow to cool slightly and cut diagonal slices on a greased cookie sheet.

*Nancy often makes this delicious rich chocolate biscotti real often for family and friends. It can be made at home for a fraction of the cost of store-bought, and it is so much better. It goes great with a cup of coffee for breakfast or with a cup of tea in the afternoon.*

## Italian Biscotti

| | |
|---|---|
| 5 | tbsp. soft butter |
| 1 ¼ | cup sugar |
| 4 | eggs, 1 at a time |
| 1 ½ | tsp vanilla extract |
| 1 ½ | tsp. anise extract |
| 4 | cups flour |
| 1 ½ | tsp. baking powder |
| 1 | tsp.  salt |
| 1 | cup chopped nuts |

Blend first two ingredients until smooth and creamy.  Mix these next three together.  Form dough into 2 or 3 flat loaves on greased baking sheet.  Bake at 350 degrees for 10-15 minutes.  Cut into diagonal strips.  Return to oven 5-10 minutes more.

*This Biscotti recipe  can be enjoyed by non-chocolate lovers, if there are any out there.  Nancy's neighbors love them and shares them at Christmas time.*

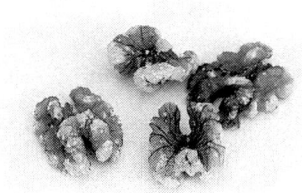

## Katie's Shortbread

2    sticks butter
1    cup confectionary sugar
1    tsp. vanilla
2    cups flour
½   cup finely chopped pecans

Cream soft butter with sugar, work in by hand the flour and add vanilla and nuts.  Mix well.   Place on wax paper and roll into a 2" round log roll and cut in half.  Chill overnight.  Preheat oven to 350 degrees.  Cut roll into ¼ inches  round and bake for 15-18 minutes on ungreased cookie sheet.

*Maggie likes to have these shortbread cookies around all the time. They are great with coffee or afternoon tea.  She also makes them for all the family at Christmas.*

## Ham and Cheese Biscuits

1    pkg. sunbeam dinner rolls
2    dashes Worcestershire sauce
2    squirts of mustard
¼   cup butter softened
1    tbsp. poppy seeds
Ham slices
Swiss cheese slices

Remove the dinner rolls from their tin. Cut long ways down the middle so that you have a top and a bottom. Put bottom half of rolls back into tin. Mix butter, Worcestershire, poppy seeds and mustard in a bowl. Spread mixture on bottom layer. Layer bottom half with ham, then Swiss, then ham again. Spread mixture on top and bottom of top layer. Place top half back into tin so as to cover the ham and Swiss. In a preheated 350 degree oven, bake until cheese has melted and the tops of the rolls are crisp to the touch. Remove and cut along pre-cut bun marks. Place a tooth pick in each and serve at parties.

*Five stars for a quick, easy, anytime snack or dinner for a busy family. This recipe is so easy, the husband could show off some cooking talent. They are outrageously addictive. Great dish for buffet and popular with the young folk.*

## Monkey Bread

2    cans biscuits cut in ¼'s
2    sticks of melted butter
5    tsp. of cinnamon
1 ½  cups sugar

   Mix cinnamon and sugar in a Bundt dish.  Layer  biscuits. Sprinkle cinnamon and sugar.  Pour melted butter over top.  Bake for 35 minutes at 400 degrees.

*Shannon has made this monkey bread many times for children's Sunday school classes.  Young people gravitate to this treat.*

"
*I am sure that never was a people, who had more reason to acknowledge a Divine interposition in their affairs, than those of the United States; and I should be pained to believe that they have forgotten that agency, which was so often manifested during our Revolution, or that they failed to consider the omnipotence of that God who is alone able to protect them.*
- George Washington
"

## Old Fashioned Dumplings

1 ½   cups all purpose flour
2     tsp. baking powder
½     tsp. salt
½     cup chicken broth
2     tbsp. vegetable oil
2     quarts broth

      Combine flour, baking powder and salt. Add ½ cup broth and oil. Stir until dry ingredients are moistened. Turn dough out on floured surface, and form into a ball. Roll dough to 1/16 inch thickness. Cut size wanted. Drop flat dumplings into boiling broth. Cover and cook 10 -15 minutes or until tender. Cooked chicken may be added to dumpling mixture.

*This recipe has been passed down through several generations of Maggie's family. Her mother knew exactly how long to work her dough so that the dumplings would stay firm when cooked and not become mushy. It may take trial and error to get them down pat. Most men love chicken and dumplings, so surprise him with a pot full and make his day.*

## Sour Cream Baby Biscuits

1    cup sour cream
2    cups self-rising flour
1    cup butter, melted

Blend sour cream into flour and add butter and stir until blended.  Pour into miniature muffin tins until 2/3 full.  Cook at 400 degrees for 15 minutes.

*You will lovvvvve these light and fluffy biscuits.  Serve them to your husband and you will make him a happy camper.*

## **Sour Cream Cornbread**

1    cup self-rising cornmeal
2    eggs
1    (83/4 oz.) can cream style corn
1    cup sour cream
½   cup salad oil

      Combine all ingredients.  Mix well.  Pour into a greased 9 inch pan.  Bake at 400 degrees for 20 to 30 minutes.

*Living in the South, you need to have cornbread with fresh greens, good winter soups and buttermilk.  Maggie's mother made this recipe for the family on days  she did not make biscuits.*

## Stir-and-Roll Biscuits

2 ¼   cups all-purpose soft-wheat flour
1       tbsp. baking powder
1       tsp. salt
2/3    cup milk
½       cup vegetable oil
        Wax paper

     Preheat oven to 475 degrees.  Sift together first 3 ingredients.
Stir in mild and oil, using a fork until dough leaves the sides of the
bowl and forms a ball.  Turn dough out onto lightly floured wax paper.  Knead 8 to 10 times.  Roll or pat dough into a ½ -inch-thick
rectangle (about 8 x 6 ½ inches).  Cut with a 2-inch round cutter,
rerolling scraps as needed.  Place 3/4-inch apart on a lightly greased
jelly-roll pan.  Bake at 475 degrees for 10 to 12 minutes or until
lightly browned.

*This is a good recipe for using wheat flour.  The biscuits are light
and fluffy as well as enjoyable.*

## Vidalia Onion Cornbread

¼    cup butter
1      large Vidalia onion, chopped
1      (7.5oz.) cornbread mix
1      cup sour cream
1/3  cup milk
1      large egg, beaten
¼    tsp. salt
1  cup cheese

Sauté onion in butter 5 minutes or until tender. Do not brown. Stir in cornbread. Mix ½ cup cheese and next 4 ingredients. Coat 8 inch pan with Pam and then pour mixture into it. Bake at 450 degrees for 25 minutes. Sprinkle evenly with remaining ½ cup cheese. Bake 5 minutes or until done. Check with wooden pick. Cool.

*Any recipe that calls for Vidalia or Glennville onions just has to be good. A wonderful indulgence for a special meal - a good change for cornbread. Enjoy!*

Fed by Grace

# Entrees
## Poultry, Meats and Seafood

Fried chicken was the earlier fare for Sunday Dinners, especially when the Preacher was to grace our table. Turkey was reserved for Thanksgiving and Christmas. Now, turkey is available the year round and is no longer just a holiday bird. Chicken is one of the most versatile meats and can be served in a variety of ways. Some outstanding recipes have been contributed for this cookbook. An old rhyme went this way "Some have meat and cannot eat, and some would eat but have no meat, but we have meat and we can eat, so let the Lord be thankful". Many of the tender cuts of meat we enjoy today were not common in the earlier years. Ham and Pork were favorites in the earlier days as well as lots of wild game such as venison, goose and others. Today refrigerated trucks bring the harvest of the sea to local stores. All of this make it possible to have crisp fried catfish or oysters on the half shell, fried shrimp and scallops. The selection is great and varied enough to please the most discriminating palate. Fish fries are still a delightful informal way to entertain especially if you have plenty of hot hush puppies.

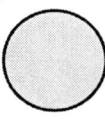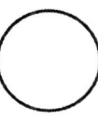

## Baked Chicken

4   chicken breasts (equivalent 6 dark pieces)
1    tbsp. French onion soup
¼  cup cranberry sauce
¼  cup French dressing

      Marinate chicken with soup, sauce and dressing overnight. Bake in greased casserole for 45 minutes at 350 degrees or until done.

*Many chicken recipes were submitted for this cookbook. We were unable to taste-test them all but we did review all very carefully and hope that we are offering you the very best. This one is very easy to make and can be done quickly. Serve with side dish and salad and you will have a happy family.*

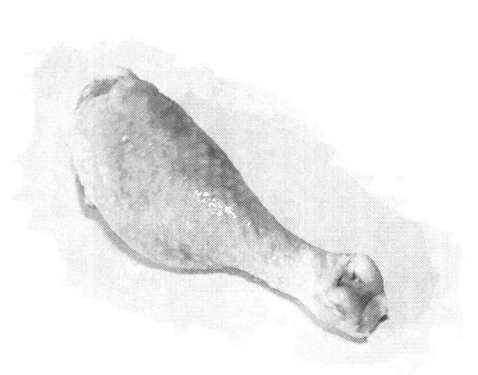

## Beef Stroganoff Over Buttered Noodles

2  lbs sirloin steak ( salt & pepper to taste)
1  stick of butter
3  cups beef stock
1  carrot, chopped
6  sprigs fresh thyme
7  tbsp. extra virgin olive oil
2  tbsp. cognac
½  lb. mushrooms, sliced
12 cloves of garlic, minced (or to taste)
½  lb. baby bella mushrooms, sliced
2  shallots, finely chopped

1  lb. extra broad egg noodles
2  tbsp freshly chopped parsley
8  oz. sour cream
2  cups heavy cream
3  tbsp. Dijon mustard
2  tbsp. each of A-1 sauce & Worcestershire sauce

Cube the sirloin steak.  Season with salt and pepper.  Put 2 tablespoons of butter and 1 tablespoon of olive oil in very hot large skillet.  Cook sirloin very fast browning both sides (about 2 minutes total).  Remove and set aside.  In same pan add ½ of cognac, 2/3 of shallots, 2/3 of minced garlic, 3 sprigs of thyme and chopped carrot, and any juices from cooked steak. After garlic and shallots have become translucent , add 3 cups of beef stock, 1 cup at a time, reducing over high heat each time until juice is reduced to 1 cup.  Strain this beef stock into a bowl and set aside.  Boil egg noodles per package directions (less 1 min.).  Drain and add 4 tbsps butter to noodles and stir.   In the same pan add 6 tbsps. of butter and 4-6 tbsps. of oil and bring back to high heat .  Add remaining garlic, shallots and thyme and cook until translucent.  Add mushrooms and cook until very tender.  Remove mushrooms from pan and add 2 cups of heavy cream and reduced beef stock and cook over med. high heat until liquid thickens. Remove  sauce  from pan and  save.  In same pan, add mustard, A-1 sauce and Worcestershire sauce and add back saved cream sauce and add sour cream until sauce is very thick.  Add back mushrooms and beef and any liquids from the dishes they were set aside in.  Combine buttered egg noodles and serve immediately.

*This is the original recipe from Tyler Florence as modified by Granville "Trey" Alley.  Trey prepared this dish for one of our Christmas Dinners  at  Lakeside Church and we can all vouch that it was very delicious.*

## Beef Stroganoff

| | |
|---|---|
| 1-1/2 | lbs sirloin steak, cubed |
| 2 | tbsp flour |
| ½ | tsp. salt & pepper to taste |
| 2 | tbsp. olive oil |
| 1 | 101/2oz can beef consommé |
| 3 | tbsp. Worcestershire sauce |
| 3 | tbsp. catsup |
| 2 | tbsp. Dijon mustard |
| 2 | shallots, finely chopped |
| ½ | lbs. mushrooms |
| 8 | oz. sour cream |

Dredge steak cubes , seasoned with salt and pepper, in flour. In skillet, brown steak cubes in olive oil over med. high heat. Add beef consommé, Worcestershire sauce, catsup, mustard and shallots. Cover and cook over low heat for about 2 hours. Add mushrooms last 15 minutes. Just before serving, add sour cream. Serve over cooked noodles or white rice.

*Another great recipe from the plantation cooks in Albany, Ga. This is an excellent dish to serve at a dinner party along with green vegetables, congealed salad and a light dessert.*

# Beef Tenderloin with Mushroom Sauce

5   lb. Beef Tenderloin, whole or cut into filets
4   tbsp.  Butter
1   clove Garlic, minced
8   oz. fresh  mushrooms, sliced
1   tsp. Dijon-style mustard
½   cup dry red wine
¼   cup beef bouillon
Pinch dried thyme and basil
Salt and pepper to taste

Place whole tenderloin in glass baking dish at 350 degrees for 20 minutes per pound.  Use meat thermometer to reach desired doneness (140 is rare meat).  If using filets, cook over medium-high heat in heavy skillet in a little butter.

Allow 3 minutes per side, turning only once.

## Mushroom Sauce
Melt 4 tbsp. butter in skillet.  Sauté garlic clove and mushrooms until mushrooms are tender.  Add remaining ingredients and simmer over low heat about 20 minutes.  If thicker gravy desired, add  flour with water and whisk into sauce.
Serve tenderloin with sauce.

*Maggie offers this recipe for tenderloin beef lovers.  This will truly make you flip over.  The mushroom sauce adds to the taste. Deceptively simple until slicing reveals the riches inside.*

## Beef Tips in Crock Pot

     Stew beef, any amount
1   pkg. Lipton onion soup
1   can golden mushroom soup
½  cup red wine
1   can mushrooms, drained

     Mix all together in crock pot and cook "all day" on low.  Serve over rice or noodles.

*Tam offers this for busy mothers.  Put it on in the morning before going to work and it is ready to serve when you get home.  A dish that the entire family will dig into.  What can be any better than good beef tips served over rice and topped with rich gravy?   With a green vegetable and salad, you will have a feast.*

## Calzones

1    lb. ground meat
1    lb. sausage
1    lb. cooked/boiled ham
2    cans Pizza dough
1    bell pepper, chopped
½   onion, chopped
1    small jar sliced mushrooms
1    8oz. container ricotta cheese
1    8oz . bag shredded pizza cheese
1    8oz. bag shredded mozzarella cheese
2    8oz. jars pizza sauce with pepperoni

Preheat oven to 425 degrees.  Grease 13x9 pan with pam. Cook hamburger meat and drain grease well.  Cook sausage and drain grease well.  Unroll one of the pizza crust and line bottom of pan with it.  Put in meats first then ricotta cheese.  Next put in veggies and pizza sauce.  Then layer remaining cheeses.  Top with second unrolled pizza crust.  Cook for about 14 – 18 minutes or until brown.  Let stand for about 10 minutes and then cut and serve.

***helpful hints***:  Leave pizza crust in fridge until needed as it will unroll easier.  Also you can put anything you want in your calzone.

*Damaris shares her husband's favorite recipe.  He cooks this for the family often and has to prepare enough to feed a growing teenage boy and girl.  This dish is great when friends pop in right at eating time.*

> *Calzones are a folded or stuffed pizza turnover made with a pizza crust and stuffed with different types of meat and cheeses.*

## Carolina Barbequed Pork

2    onions, quartered
2    tbsp. brown Sugar
1    tbsp. Paprika
2    tsp. salt
½   tsp. black pepper
1    (4 to 6 pound) boneless pork butt or shoulder roast
4    tsp. Worcestershire sauce
1 ½ tsp. crushed red pepper flakes
1 ½ tsp. sugar
½   tsp. dry mustard
½   tsp. garlic salt
¼   tsp. cayenne
¼   cup cider vinegar
Hamburger buns and coleslaw, optional

Place onions in stoneware. Combine brown sugar, paprika, salt and pepper. Rub over roast. Place roast over onion. Combine vinegar, Worcestershire sauce, red pepper flakes, sugar, mustard, garlic salt, and cayenne. Stir to mix well. Drizzle about one third of this mixture over roast. Cover and refrigerate remaining vinegar mixture. Cover stone ware and cook on low 8 to 10 hours (High 4 to 6 hours). Drizzle about one third reserved vinegar mixture over roast during last half hour of cooking. Remove meat and onions, drain. Chop or shred meat and chop onions. Serve meat and onions on buns. If desired, top sandwiches with coleslaw. Pass remaining vinegar mixture to drizzle over sandwiches.

*There are as many barbeque recipes as there are small towns in the South. It is known as the most famous dish to emerge from camp-fires and cabins of early Americans. Amy submitted this one for us to try, and she thinks it may become one of your favorites.*

## Chicken and Stuffing Bake

4    cups herb seasoned stuffing
6    boneless chicken breasts
1    can cream of mushroom soup
1/3  cup milk
1    tbsp. chopped fresh parsley
½    cup boiling water
1    tbsp butter
Paprika

      Mix stuffing with ½ cup boiling water and 1 tbsp. margarine. Spoon stuffing across center of 2 qt. shallow baking dish. Place chicken on each side. Sprinkle chicken with paprika. Mix soup, milk and parsley. Pour over chicken. Bake covered at 400 degrees for 15 minutes. Then uncover and bake 15 minutes longer or until chicken is done.

*Audrey certainly knows how to cook those one-dish casseroles. This one has been tested often and the recipe is always asked for.*

## Chicken & Rice Casserole

1     whole chicken or chicken pieces  to equal
1     can cream of chicken soup
1     can cream of mushroom with garlic Soup
1     can French onion soup
1 ½ cans of warm water
2     sticks of butter
2     cups basmati rice ( regular rice may be substituted)
Seasoning of choice

Simmer chicken in seasoned water.  Debone and tear or cut into bite-size pieces and set aside.  Whisk together the three soups and warm water with seasoning of choice.  Melt butter in a casserole dish and spread uncooked rice evenly over the butter.  Top butter and rice with chicken pieces.  Pour soup mixture over all.  Cover with foil and bake at 325 degrees for 1 hour.

*Nancy is a great chef in the casserole department, had to be with three sons and a husband to feed.  We think you will enjoy this dish.  After you try this one, you may want to also try Christian's recipe on page 122.*

## Chicken Casserole

4   boneless and skinless chicken breasts, cooked
1   can cream of chicken soup
1   large container of sour cream
1   stick of butter
1   roll of Ritz crackers

Mix in casserole baking dish the cocked chicken, soup and sour cream and bake for 20 minutes at 400 degrees.  Crush crackers while still in the package. Melt the butter in a pan and add crushed crackers.  Top casserole with cracker mixture and bake for 10 more minutes.

*Shannon considers this a good family dish,  especially for that busy mother on the go.  Even your "pickiest" child will enjoy this and it can be prepared quickly.*

## Chicken Divan

2    pkg. broccoli florets, cooked and drained
4    large chicken breasts, cooked and chopped
2    cans cream of chicken soup
2    tbsp. lemon juice
1    cup mayonnaise
1    cup grated cheese
Crushed multigrain Saltines

In a 3 qt. casserole dish spread broccoli, then sprinkle with lemon juice.  Place chicken over broccoli and sprinkle with lemon juice.  Make soup mixture of mayonnaise and 2 tbsp. lemon juice and pour over the chicken.  Spread 1 cup of grated cheese over soup mixture.  Add crushed multigrain saltines and spread over the cheese.  Bake uncovered 25 minutes at 350 degrees or until bubbles in the middle.

*This recipe was given to Nancy by her special friend, Lorene. Nancy will vouch for this being an enjoyable meal within itself.  She has often prepared it for family and for special occasions that call for a casserole.*

> *God promises a safe landing, not a calm passage.*

## Chicken Enchilada

1    whole chicken, (cooked and cubed into bite size)
1    large onion, sautéed
2    10-pack burrito size tortillas
2    cans cream of mushroom soup
1    can cream of chicken soup
1    bag of shredded cheese (4 cups or better)
Taco seasoning

      Mix in large bowl the chicken, the taco seasoning, the onion and 1 can of cream of mushroom soup, half of the chicken soup. Then add cheese to taste (around 2 cups) and set aside. Heat frying pan sprayed with cooking spray and warm a tortilla. Remove and fill with the chicken mixture, and repeat until all tortillas are filled. Add filled Tortillas to a baking dish coated with cooking spray. Cover with balance of chicken soup and any chicken mixture left over. Cover with cheese and then bake at 350 degrees until heated through. Cheese should be melted and bubbly.

*This recipe was passed on to Tam by an Internet West Coast friend named De. For those enchilada lovers, this is a must.*

## Chicken 'N Dumplings

1     chicken
3-4  chicken bouillon cubes (to taste)
2     cups self-rising flour
¼    cup melted butter
¾    cup milk

Take skin off of chicken and boil until done.  Remove  meat and discard the bones.   Add bouillon cubes and pepper if desired.  Set aside.  Make biscuits with flour, melted butter, and milk.  Mix well and roll out on a floured board and cut into strips.  Drop biscuits strips into chicken and broth.  Simmer until dumplings are cooked (just a few minutes).  May need to add some  flour and water shaken in a container to thicken the broth slightly.

*In the South, there is nothing like a big pot of chicken and dumplings waiting for a  church crowd when they have  a  5th Sunday "dinner on the ground".  Nancy's recipe is considered one of the best.  The secret to good dumplings is knowing how long to work the dough.*

## Chicken Parmesan

4    boneless and skinless chicken breast
1    egg,  slightly beaten
½    cup bread crumbs
2    tbsps. butter
1 ¾ cups spaghetti sauce with mushrooms
1 Tbsp. parmesan cheese   1/2 cup shredded mozzarella
¼    tsp. chopped parsley

      Use palm of hand to flatten chicken.  Dip chicken into egg then coat with crumbs.  Cook in a skillet over medium heat in hot butter until brown on both sides.  Add spaghetti sauce and reduce heat.  Cover and simmer 10 minutes.  Sprinkle with cheese and parsley.  Cover and simmer 5 minutes.


*Robyn, Nancy's daughter-in-law, prepares this good and hearty dish for her family.*

Fed by Grace

## Chicken Parisienne in Crock Pot

6   chicken breasts
1   can cream of chicken or mushroom soup
14  oz. can sliced or button mushrooms
½  cup dry white wine
I   cup sour cream
¼  cup flour mixed in sour cream

   Pour all of the above over the chicken breasts, covering completely.  Salt and pepper on mixture.  Sprinkle with paprika.  Cook on low 6-8 hours

*DeAnn feels that crock pot cooking can be an answer for today's busy cooks.  This is outstanding and can be served with rice and salad for a complete meal.*

> The safest place to be is within the will of God.

## Chicken Pie

6     chicken breasts, cooked and cubed
1¾ cups broth
1     can cream of celery soup
1     stick butter, melted
1     cup self-rising flour
¾     cup milk
1     large can Veg-All or 1 small bag frozen Veg-All, optional
Salt and pepper

　　　Place chicken in 9x13 dish. Pour broth over chicken, add vegetables (if desired), then pour soup over all.  Season with salt and pepper.  In a separate bowl mix butter, flour and milk together. Pour evenly over ingredients in baking dish. Bake at 350 degrees for 40 minutes or until bubbly and crust is brown.

*Audrey shares this recipe with us because it has been a favorite of the Beal family for many past years.   This is another one of those "southern traditions".*

## Chicken Strata

6    slices white bread
2    cups cooked chicken, diced
½    cup chopped onion
½    cup finely chopped Celery
½    cup mayonnaise
¾    tsp. salt
2    beaten eggs
1 ½ cups milk
1    (10 1/2 oz) condensed cream of mushroom soup
½    cup shredded sharp process American cheese

Cube 2 slices of bread and trim crusts from remaining 4 slices bread (cut up crusts). Place cubed bread and crusts in bottom of 8 x 8 x 2 inch baking dish. Reserve 4 trimmed bread slices to be used later. Combine 2 cups diced cooked chicken, ½ cup chopped onion, ½ cup finely chopped celery, ½ cup mayonnaise, and ¾ teaspoon salt. Spoon over bread cubes. Arrange reserved bread slices atop the chicken mixture. Combine 2 beaten eggs and 1 ½ cups milk. Pour over all. Cover and chill 1 hour or preferably overnight. Stir one 10 ½ oz. can condensed cream of mushroom soup and spoon over top. Bake in slow oven (325 degrees) about 1 hour or till set. Sprinkle ½ cup shredded sharp process American cheese over top last few minutes of baking. Makes 6 servings.

*When Maggie first met Harold, this was the first dinner recipe he prepared for her. It was so impressive, Maggie got the idea he could cook. After they were married, she realized this was only one of two entree dishes he has ever cooked. The other one, also shared in this cookbook, is scalloped oysters.*

# Chicken With Porcini Mushrooms

1    oz. dried porcini mushrooms, soaked for 30 minutes in 3 cups very hot water
6    boneless, skinless chicken breasts
¼   cup  clarified butter
⅓   cup chopped shallots (2 large)
1    tbsp. minced garlic (3 cloves)
1    cup Madeira wine
1    cup (8 ounces) crème fraiche
     (lt. sour cream/French)
1    cup heavy cream
2    tbsp. freshly squeezed lemon juice
Kosher salt and pepper
All-purpose flour, for dredging

> *A nickel will get you on the subway, but garlic will get you a seat.*
> *(Old N.Y. Proverb)*

Preheat the oven to 375 degrees . Soak the mushrooms for 30 minutes in 3 cups of hot water. Lift the mushrooms carefully from the hot water in order to leave any grit behind in the liquid. Rinse a few times to be sure all the grittiness is gone. Discard the liquid and dry the mushrooms lightly with paper towels. Set aside. Season chicken with salt and pepper. Dredge in flour and shake off the excess. Heat half the butter in a large pan and cook the chicken in 2 batches over medium-low heat until browned on both sides, 8 to 10 minutes. Remove to an ovenproof casserole. Add the rest of the butter to the pan along with the shallots, drained mushrooms, and garlic. Sauté over medium heat for 2 minutes, tossing and stirring constantly. Pour the wine into the pan and reduce the liquid by half over high heat, 2 to 4 minutes. Add the crème fraiche, cream, lemon juice, 1 teaspoon salt, and ¾ teaspoon pepper. Boil until the mixture starts to thicken, 5 to 10 minutes. Pour the sauce over the chicken and bake for 12 minutes, or until the chicken is heated through. To make ahead, refrigerate the chicken and sauce in the casserole and reheat slowly on top of the stove.

*This dish proves that Doris is truly an outstanding cook. If you can't find crème fraise, you can make it by mixing equal amounts of heavy cream and sour cream thoroughly together and letting sit until the mixture thickens. Clarified butter is butter that is heated slowly and the fat that rises to the top is skimmed off.*

## Chili

1   lb.  hamburger meat
1   can dark kidney beans
1   can light kidney beans
1   small onion
2  tbsp. chili powder
Salt & pepper to taste

      Brown and drain hamburger meat. Drain beans. Finely chop onion. Combine all ingredients and mix well. You can cook in two ways: on stove or in crock pot.  If on the stove, cook on medium heat until beans are soft. Stir frequently.  If in crock pot, cook on low for about 3 hours. Stir frequently.  After it has cooked for about 15 minutes, taste and add more chili powder if needed.

*Damaris says this is not a fancy chili recipe but is very good and she has been making it this way since she was 13 years old.  This is a favorite when the weather is turning cooler.*

## CQ's Crab Cakes

| | |
|---|---|
| 1 | lb. lump crabmeat, de-shelled |
| 1 | lb. Dijon mustard (Grey Poupon) |
| 1-1/2 | tbsp. mayonnaise |
| 1 | tbsp. fresh lemon juice |
| 1 | tbsp. Worcestershire sauce |
| ½ | tsp. Old Bay seasoning |
| ¼ | tsp. black pepper |
| ½ | cup ground Ritz cracker crumbs |
| 2 | cups flour |
| ¼ | stick (2tbsp.) butter |

Mix well all ingredients except cracker crumbs. Add crumbs gradually until mixture is loose but firm enough to hold together. Form into 8 crab cakes. Lightly coat each crab cake with flour. Sauté in butter in a pre-heated sauté pan until golden brown on each side. Bake at 400 degrees for 6-8 minutes. For the Lemon-Horseradish Sauce: In a sauce pan, reduce 2 cups heavy whipping cream, 1 cup white wine and 3 tbsp. fresh lemon juice by half, ad 2 tbsp. horseradish and ¼ tsp. salt. Pour the sauce on the plate and place crab cakes on top. Garnish with chopped fresh parsley. Yield: four servings.

*Maggie was given this special recipe from CQ's in Harbor Town, Hilton Head. They are the best Crab Cakes made in the low country area. They are easy to make and especially good! This is considered one of the signature dishes of the Low country.*

> *When the fishing boats would come in to the docks, the islanders would be waiting in line for freshly caught blue crab to make the above succulent crab cakes.*

## Crab Quiche

½      cup mayonnaise
2      tbsp. flour
2      eggs beaten
½      cup milk
2      cans crabmeat (or salmon), or 1 can 14.75 oz.
1/3   cup green onions
1      tbsp. chopped parsley
2      cups shredded Swiss cheese
1      unbaked deep dish pastry shell

Mix together mayo, flour, eggs, milk. Stir in crab or salmon, onions, parsley and cheese. Spoon into shell. Bake @ 350 degrees for 1 hour.

*Nancy has prepared this dish for some of our get-togethers. It is delicious served with either crab meat or fresh salmon. It can be that perfect dish to serve on a buffet. Very appetizing.*

## Creamed Chicken and Biscuits

2    cups chopped cooked chicken
½    cup milk
½    tsp. poultry seasoning
¼    tsp. pepper
1    can of cream of chicken soup (undiluted)
1    (10 oz.) package frozen mixed veggies
1    (6 oz.) can buttermilk biscuits

Combine first 6 ingredients in a sauce pan.  Cook over medium heat 10-15 minutes or until thoroughly heated, stirring often. Meanwhile bake biscuits according to package directions.  Split hot biscuits in half.  Spoon chicken mixture over biscuit halves.

*What can be any better than chicken and biscuits.  Sounds yummy. This recipe, given to Nancy by her daughter-in-law, has been a favorite in the family for a long time.*

*I believe in the sun even if it isn't shining. I believe in love even when I am alone. I believe in God even when He is silent.*

## Deep Dish Spaghetti Pie

6    oz. uncooked spaghetti
2    eggs slightly beaten
¼   cup grated parmesan cheese
1    lb. ground beef
¼   cup chopped onion (optional)
1    (14oz) jar of spaghetti sauce
1    (11oz) can of vacuum-packed whole kernel corn, drained
1    green bell pepper, cut into rings
1    cup shredded mozzarella cheese

Cook spaghetti to desired doneness as directed on the package. Drain, rinse with hot water. Heat oven to 350 degrees. Grease 10 inch pie pan or 9 x 13 rectangle pan. Combine cooked spaghetti, eggs and Parmesan cheese; toss lightly. Place in greased pan. Press evenly into pan to form a crust. Set aside. In a large skillet, brown ground beef with onion until beef is thoroughly cooked. Drain. Stir in spaghetti sauce and corn. Spoon mixture evenly over crust. Top with bell peppers and sprinkle with mozzarella cheese. Bake at 350 degrees for 25 to 30 minutes. Let stand for 5 minutes before serving. Serves 6.

*April learned to cook this dish while in college and would make it with friends. It is easy, inexpensive, and tastes great. Any leftovers are also good. It is perfect for any college student or busy mom!*

## Deer Burger  Casserole

1    lb. ground deer (or hamburger for a different taste), browned
1    lg. sweet onion,  sautéed
1    lg. can cream of mushroom soup
1    can of English peas
1/2  bag of egg noodles,  cooked and drained
1/2  cup of Worcestershire sauce
4    cups of shredded cheddar cheese (retain 1  1/2 cup for the top)

Combine all ingredients,  except the 1 ½ cup of cheese for the top,  into a large pan that has been sprayed with cooking spray for easier clean up.  Spread the remaining cheese on top and then bake at 350 degrees until cheese is melted and bubbly.

*This recipe was handed down to Tam by her Mom who cooked by making do with what she had.  Making do is about taking whatever is a at hand and using it for your advantage.  This deer casserole will certainly be a treat on your dinner table.*

## Chicken with Rice

**L.O.A. Kids**
Lake Oconee Academy
Thanksgiving Recipes

1   big rice bag
50  lbs. of chicken
1   slice butter

First, cook the rice. Then bake the chicken. Then mix it up. Melt the butter. And put it on the chicken. Then put it in the oven for 40 minutes. Then eat it. I eat it all the time at my Tita and Tito's house.

*Christian is a first grade student at Lake Oconee Academy and this was his recipe in the First Grade Thanksgiving recipe book.*

## Green Pepper Steaks

1   lb.  top round steak
1   tbsp. oil
1   clove garlic, crushed
2   onions, coarsely chopped, divided
1   cup Coca-Cola
1   large green pepper
6   oz.  mushroom slices
Salt and pepper to taste
Tomato slices for garnish

Cut the meat into ½ inch strips after trimming off any fat.  In a large skillet heat the oil, add the meat with garlic and brown  well.  Add half the chopped onion.  Add the salt, pepper, curry powder and Coca-Cola.  Simmer, covered, for 1 hour.  Add more liquid if needed.  Cut green pepper in thin strips.  In a small pan brown the pepper with the remaining onion  in a small amount of oil.  Add to the steak.  Stir in mushrooms.  Simmer 20 minutes more.  Top with tomato slices.

*Amy says this is a special recipe because it is made with the famous "Coca-Cola".  It is a favorite of her family, and she knows that any-one who tries this dish will be pleasantly pleased.*

## Ham and Swiss Strata

8     slices white bread, crust removed and cubed
1 ½ cup diced ham
1 ½ cups Swiss cheese, shredded
8     eggs
2     cups milk
4     tbsp melted butter
½     tsp dry mustard
1     small chopped onion
1     cup sliced mushrooms
Salt to taste

     Butter a 9 x 13 x 2 inch ovenproof dish.  Layer the dish with bread, then ham, then Swiss cheese.  Whisk together the eggs, milk, butter, dry mustard and salt.  Pour over bread mixture and cover.  Refrigerate overnight.  Uncover and bake for 50 minutes at 350 degrees.  Let stand for 5 minutes.  Cut in squares and serve.

*Strata dishes are a favorite for breakfast buffets and a treat for house guests. Cooking this recipe provides a pleasant aroma in the kitchen early in the morning.  It is delicious when served with fresh fruits and blueberry muffins.*

## Harvest Chicken Chowder

2   lbs. boneless, skinless chicken breast (diced)
6   cups  chicken broth
½   tsp. salt
½   tsp. black pepper
6   potatoes, peeled and cubed
3   carrots, diced
½   cup  celery, diced
½   cup onion, finely chopped
1   can sliced mushroom, drained (4oz )
1   pkg. frozen whole kernel corn, thawed
1   can cream of chicken soup
4   slices cooked bacon, crumbled
1   cup heavy whipping cream
3   tbsp. all-purpose flour
1/3  cup water
Parsley sprigs for garnish

     In a 4 or 5 quart pot, bring broth, salt, pepper, potatoes, carrots, celery and onion to a boil over medium heat.  Reduce heat to low.  Cover and simmer for 30 minutes until carrots are tender.  Stir in diced chicken, mushrooms and corn.  Cook over low heat for 10 to 15 minutes until chicken  is done, stirring often.  Stir in soup, bacon and cream.  Heat through.  In a small bowl, stir together flour and water until smooth.  Stir into pot.  Heat over low heat until chowder thickens slightly, stirring
often.

*This is a good way to prepare chicken with good vegetables and results in a meal in one pot. It will be enjoyed when served with garlic bread and green salad.*

## Hot Chicken Salad Casserole

2-3   cups cooked and diced chicken
2      hard boiled eggs, chopped
1      can cream of chicken soup
¾     cup mayonnaise
2      cups celery, chopped
¼     cup chopped pecans
2      cups dried stuffing mix
Salt and pepper

Mix chicken soup with mayonnaise and add to chicken mixture. Bake at 325 degrees for 30 to 40 minutes.

*This recipe is from Nettie, a neighbor of Nancy. Nancy would like everyone to try this special dish. It has become one of her stand-bys.*

## Maple-Bourbon Pork Loin

1    pork loin
1    tbsp. Coarse ground pepper
1    cup maple-bourbon glaze (Recipe below)
        Mix 2 cups water and 2 cups of sugar and bring to boil.  Add 1
tbsp. corn starch       dissolved in cold water to thicken and allow to
cook for a few minutes until sauce          thickens.  Stir in 1 tbsp.
Vermont maple syrup, 1 tsp. of maple extract and ¼ cup        of
Bourbon.  Remove from  heat and allow to cool to thicken to glaze.
1    tbsp. Coarse salt
2    cups marinated dried fruits (Recipe below)

Combine the following ingredients and let soak overnight:
1 cup raisins, 3 cups dried apricots, ¼ cup golden raisins, ¼ cup
dried papaya, ¼ cup dried pineapple, ¼ cup dry cherries, 1 tbsp.
fresh chopped parsley, ¼ cup Bourbon,  1/8 tsp. cayenne pepper, ¾
cup apple cider, ¾ cup packed dark brown sugar,  and dusting of
salt and pepper.  Roast for 30 minutes before serving at 350  degrees or until all liquid is absorbed and glaze forms.  Serve warm
over sliced pork.

Salt and pepper the Pork loin and place on a roasting pan.  Brush on
maple-bourbon glaze before cooking (marinate in glaze for 2 hours
before cooking).  Cook  pork to desired level of doneness, basting occasionally while in the oven.  Serve slices of pork loin over dried
fruits.

*Karen was given this recipe by a friend who got it from her
grandmother in Scotland.  She was an excellent cook and her
family learned to cook from her.  When this recipe was given to
Karen, it  was written in the grandmother's  own handwriting.
Karen claims this as an outstanding way to prepare pork.  It will
taste as good as it looks.*

## Mexicali Chicken With Rice Or Burritos

| | |
|---|---|
| 1 | lb. boneless skinless chicken breast |
| 1 | 15oz can chili (beef)( look for low-fat brands) |
| 3 | oz. fat free cream cheese |
| ¼ | cup mild 'thick n' chunky' salsa |
| 1 | cup shredded cheddar cheese |

Tortillas or cooked rice to serve

In 12 inch non-stick skillet cook chicken over medium heat until fully cooked. Remove chicken and cut into ¼ inch strips, cut strips into ½ inch strips. Return to skillet; add chili, cream cheese and salsa. Heat over medium heat stirring constantly until cheese is completely dissolved. Sprinkle with cheddar cheese, cover and cook 2-3 minutes. Serve over cooked rice or roll into tortillas like burritos and serve with taco sauce on the side.

*Audrey says this is one of her simple recipes that can be just the ticket for a light supper and will serve four to six.*

## Miss Dot's Crab Au Gratin

1    lb. crab meat
3    cups white sauce (see recipe below)
2    8 oz. bar of sharp cheddar cheese (gold package)
1    cup Ritz crackers to top casserole (crushed)
White Sauce
    8    tbsp. butter
    ½    cup flour
    1    tsp. salt
    4    cups milk

    Butter a 8 x 13" casserole dish. Spread crab meat evenly in bottom of dish. Grate cheese and spread over crabmeat. Pour hot white sauce over top. Place crushed crackers over top of white sauce. Dot with butter. Bake about 30 minutes at 350 degrees until evenly browned.

## White Sauce

    Melt butter; remove from heat. Stir in flour; add salt. Return to heat and cook, stirring constantly until mixture is bubbly. Add milk slowly. Bring to a boil over medium heat, stirring frequently. Lower heat and simmer 1 to 2 minutes then let stand for 2 minutes.

*This delicious recipe was given to Maggie years ago by a dear lady, Dot Hall. She enjoyed cooking her fresh seafood caught right out her back door on the May river in Bluffton, S.C. and she shared it with all her neighbors and friends.*

## Mrs. Jetti's Chili

1   pound ground beef,  browned
1   small to medium onion,  chopped
1   tbsp. of chili powder (to taste)
Ketchup (add as needed for right consistency to spoon onto tortilla later).

    Mix all these together and cook until onions are soft.

*Tam says, "Mrs.Jettie is a fine example of a good- hearted  woman . As my Dad and Louis L'Amour would say, "she's one to ride the river with".  As a Godmother to my son, she is special to our family." Hope you enjoy her chili as well as Tam's family does.*

*Fed by Grace*

## Mushroom Quesadillas

Salsa
1/2    cup  whole pecans
3       tbsps. balsamic vinegar
2       tbsps. olive oil
1/3    cup sugar
1       tbsp. Dijon mustard
2       cups  fresh cooked or frozen cranberries
1       shallot, sliced
1       jalapeno, seeded and minced (optional)
Grated zest and juice of 1 orange
Kosher salt and freshly grated black pepper, to taste

Quesadilla
1       stick unsalted butter
1       yellow onion, coarsely chopped
1 1/2  lbs. mixed mushrooms (any you like) stems removed
1       lb. button or cremini mushrooms (sliced)
4       cloves garlic, minced
1       tsp. kosher salt
2       tbsp. Worcestershire sauce
2/3    cup dry white wine (stock may be substituted)
½      tsp. ground white pepper
8       8 inch flour tortillas
2       cups (8oz) Monterey jack cheese
3       cup (15oz) crumbled fresh goat cheese

To make salsa:  Preheat oven to 350 and roast pecans for 7-9 min.  Transfer to bowl and let cool.  Coarsely chop and set aside.  In food processor, combine vinegar, olive oil, sugar, mustard, orange zest, orange juice, salt and pepper. ..

...Process for 30 seconds then add cranberries, shallot and jalapeno and coarsely chop.  Pour salsa in bowl, refrigerate until ready to serve.  Stir in pecans just prior to serving.  In large sauté pan , melt butter over med high heat, add the onion and sauté for about 4 minutes, until translucent.  Add mushrooms, garlic, salt and Worcestershire sauce and sauté about 5 minutes.  Add the white wine and pepper and cook until liquid is absorbed, at least 5 minutes.  While mushrooms cook, coat a griddle or large skillet with cooking spray and heat over high heat, then reduce to medium.  Lay 2 tortillas on griddle or skillet and cover each with 1/4 c of Monterey jack cheese.  Evenly spread about 1/3 c mushroom mixture on one half of each tortilla and cover mushroom mixture evenly with a thin layer of crumbled goat cheese. Use a metal spatula to fold each tortilla in half and cook until lightly brown and crisp on the bottom.  Flip and cook until brown on the other side.  Transfer to a plate in a warm oven.  Repeat with remaining tortillas.  Cut each folded tortilla into 3 wedges and serve warm or at room temperature with salsa alongside.  Add pecans before serving.

*Doris says this recipe makes a great addition to a tapas bar.  The cranberry salsa adds a little extra something and would also provide some holiday flair during the season.  Doesn't this recipe just scream Texas, which is where it originated?  Makes 4-6 main servings or 24 appetizers.*

*The left over salsa may be refrigerated for up to 3 weeks. It makes a great accompaniment to roast pork.*

## Orange Roughy

Coat fish fillets with a combination of 1 tbsp milk and 1 tbsp. heavy cream.  Dust fillet lightly with flour.  Sprinkle fillets with Stubbs Chile Lime rub,  1 tsp. fresh minced garlic, pinch of seasoned salt and fresh ground pepper.  Sauté fillets in a combination of olive oil and butter (1 tbsp. each) until lightly browned on each side.  Remove fish from pan.  To the pan drippings, add ¼ cup white wine, juice from 1 lime, 1 tbsp. orange juice (more if you like), ½ tsp. pure orange oil, 1 tsp. minced garlic, 1 tbsp. butter.  Reduce this mixture to 1/3 or original volume.  Serve sauce over fillets.

*Our Titus 2 ladies love those recipes prepared by Trey (Karen's husband).  His ingredients always tend to give flavor and substance to his dishes.  Stubbs Chile Lime rub was found at Targets in Stone Mountain and the orange oil was found at the DeKalb Farmer's Market.  If you cannot find these two items, just call Trey.*

## Paprika Chicken Rolls

4   chicken breasts, boned and skinned
4   chicken thighs, boned and skinned
2   tsp. salt
1   tsp. pepper
1   tbsp. paprika
2   tbsp. flour
8   slices bacon
¼   cup water
1   clove garlic
¼   tsp. accent

    Sprinkle chicken with accent, flour, salt, pepper, and paprika. Roll each piece and wrap with bacon on the bias. Rub skillet with garlic. Brown chicken in uncovered skillet. Drain fat off and add water. Cook in covered skillet on low for 30 minutes.

*This is the chicken dish which Barbara prepared for the judges of the Mrs. America Contest in Ohio. She says it got very good raves and put her in the winner's box. She won a new gas stove for this dish.*

## Peanut Chicken

4   chicken breasts or 6 dark pieces
¼   cup peanut butter
¼   cup orange juice
1   tsp. thyme

     Marinate chicken with peanut butter, orange juice, and thyme overnight.  Bake at 350 degrees for 45-60 minutes.

*When Shannon talks about easy, she means easy with this dish. After you try it, we think you will be pleasantly surprised at the pleasing and appealing  taste.  Peanut butter will make any thing good.*

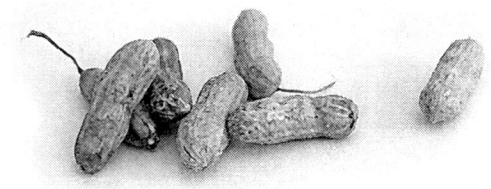

## Pecan-Crusted Catfish

4  catfish (tilapia) fillets 6 to 8 oz. each
2  tbsp. honey mustard
1  cup pecans, chopped

     Preheat oven to 450 degrees.  Line a rimmed baking pan with nonstick foil.  Finely chop pecans by hand or in food processor. Spread on a sheet of wax paper.  Put homey mustard in small cup and stir in2 tsp. water.  Brush one side of fillets with mustard mixture.  Then press into chopped pecans.  Place on baking pan.  Bake 10 to 14 minutes until pecans are lightly toasted and fish is just cooked through.  Serves 4.

*Maggie says this is a good way to prepare catfish to make it taste almost fried and eliminate the fishy smell in the kitchen while cooking. The honey gives it a very  good taste.*

*How do we kill the odor of cooking fish indoors has been a question many have asked over the years. Maggie says to open the window or just go out to eat. Seriously, we suggest that you place a cup of vinegar near where you are cooking to absorb the odor or burn a favorite scented candle.*

## Pineapple Chicken

| | |
|---|---|
| 1 or 2 | cans of pineapple chunks (1 ¼ cup pineapple juice) |
| 1 | cup sugar |
| 2 | tbsp. cornstarch |
| ¾ | cup cider vinegar |
| 1 | tbsp. soy sauce |
| ¼ | tsp. ground ginger |
| 1 | tsp. chicken bouillon |
| 2 | lb. boneless skinless chicken breast |

Preheat oven to 350°. Cut chicken into bite size pieces. Chicken can be breaded and fried or grilled, your preference. While chicken is cooking, combine pineapple juice (reserve chunks of pineapple) and all other ingredients in a boiler over med-high heat. Bring mixture to a boil. Remove from heat. When chicken is cooked place in a casserole dish, add pineapple chunks and cover with the sauce. Bake for 15 – 20 minutes to allow chicken to absorb flavors. Serve over rice.

*DeAnn says this is one of her family's favorite dishes.*

# Pineapple Chicken Cheese Melt

1   can (20 oz) slice pineapple
5   large boneless half chicken breasts
2   tbsp.  butter
1   tsp.  salt
1½  cups mayonnaise
½   cup sliced green onion (opt.)
1   tsp.  dill weed, crumbled
5   English muffins, split and toasted
1 ½ cups shredded cheddar cheese

Drain pineapple. Cut each chicken breast in half and pound flat. Sauté in butter until golden; sprinkle with salt. Combine mayonnaise, onion and dill weed. Spread ½ of mixture over muffins. Place one piece chicken on each muffin half and top with pineapple slices. Spread remaining mayonnaise mixture over tops. Sprinkle with cheese. Broil about 4 inches from heat for 3-4 minutes until cheese is bubbly and brown.
Makes 10 servings

For a lower carb version,  eliminate the muffins and place chicken into a baking dish. Spread chicken with ½ mayonnaise mixture. Place pineapple slice on top of each breast, spread with remaining mayonnaise mixture then top with cheese and finish as above.

*Audrey  has given us two ways to prepare this dish.  One using English muffins, and one without the muffins and served as a casserole.*

## Pork Chops

1   medium onion, sliced
4   center-cut Pork chops
1   can cream of mushroom soup
½  cup dry white wine
1   tsp. dried parsley
Salt to taste

Brown pork chops after sprinkling with season salt in open frying pan. Mix together soup, wine and parsley in a bowl. Add to pork chops. Simmer covered and turn pork chop occasionally. Cook for about 45 minutes or one hour. Serve with rice.

*Most of us grew up loving pork chops. Great recipe for a quick meal to prepare when everyone is on the run or for a cold winter night. A real gourmet delight.*

# Pork Loin With Red Plum Sauce

5 to 8  pound pork loin
2        tbsp. butter
¾        cup chopped onion
1        cup red plum preserves
½        cup brown sugar, packed
2/3      cup water
2        tbsp.  lemon juice
1/3      cup chili sauce
¼        cup soy sauce
2        tsp. prepared mustard
3        drops Tabasco
Garlic salt
Onion salt

Preheat oven to 325 degrees F.  Sprinkle pork generously with garlic and onion salts; place fat side up in roasting pan.  Roast at 325 degrees F, 25 minutes per pound.
If you prefer, you can place roast on rack and add little water to roasting pan. For sauce, melt butter, add onion and cook until tender.  Add remaining ingredients, simmer 15 minutes.  Pour excess fat out of baked pork, then pour about half the sauce over meat.  Cook about 20 to 30 minutes longer, basting often.  Serve extra sauce on side.

*This is one of four recipes  in this cookbook given to Maggie by her late sister, Betty.  Betty  worked  for a company that managed  several of the historical large plantations in Albany, Georgia.  She had the opportunity to enjoy many good meals prepared by the plantation cooks.  When the cooks tried to give her the recipes, the cooks would say "just add a little of this and a little of that".  These recipes have been tried and tested for sure. This dish was enjoyed by the late President Eisenhower on his many visits to one of the plantations.*

## Perfect Roast Beef

1    (3-pound) eye-round roast, trimmed
1    (1-oz.) package dried porcini mushrooms
1    tbsp. dried green peppercorns
1    tbsp. fresh rosemary leaves
3    garlic cloves, peeled
2    tsp.  extra-virgin olive oil
¼   tsp. salt

  Remove beef and let stand at room temperature for 1 hour.
Preheat oven to 500 degrees.  Place a rack in a roasting pan.  Pulse
mushrooms, peppercorns, rosemary, and garlic in a food processor
until ground.  Rub beef with the oil.  Sprinkle with salt.  Press mushroom mixture onto beef.  Place roast in baking dish or pan.  Do not
cover or add water.  Reduce oven temperature  to 475 degrees.
Roast for 21 minutes (7 minutes  per pound)  then turn off the oven
and let the roast sit in the hot oven for 2 ½ hours  Do not open the
oven door at all during this time.   Remove from oven and carve into
thin slices.

*This is a very easy way to prepare an eye-of-round roast so that it
may be served rare or medium rare.  This recipe takes a very tough
piece of meat and makes it  so tender and delicious.  Perfect entrée
for entertaining special guests.*

# Roast Venison With Vegetables

3-5   pound venison roast
3      slices bacon
½     cup water
1      tbsp. vinegar
½     cup chopped celery
½     apple, chopped
1      carrot, diced
1      tbsp. lemon juice
1/3   cup canned mushrooms, chopped
1      beef bouillon cube
2      tbsp. cornstarch
Salt and pepper

     Rub meat with salt and pepper and flour, and sear in a little oil until brown. Put into a pot, pinning the bacon slices to top with toothpicks. Add ½ cup water and vinegar. Cover and cook in moderate oven one hour. Then add the celery, apple, carrots, raisins, mushrooms, and lemon juice. Continue baking until tender. For gravy remove the meat and part of the vegetables. Add beef bouillon and a little water. Thicken with cornstarch. Salt and pepper to taste.

*We found this a very good recipe for venison. Many who have a taste for deer meat will be pleasantly surprised with the substantial satisfying meal. This dish is tasty served over rice or large egg noodles.*

## Salmon Cakes

4    cups water
1    lemon, fresh
1    10-12 ounce Salmon filet
1/3  cup onion, chopped
1/3  cup celery, chopped
3    tsp. mayonnaise
     pinch of cayenne pepper
¾    tsp. tarragon
½    tsp garlic
¼    tsp. dry mustard
½    tsp. salt
½    tsp. black pepper
1    4-ounce pouch Idaho butter and herb dry mashed potatoes
Canola oil for frying patties

> *Salmon promotes cardiovascular health with omega-3 fats and when eaten twice per week will make the blood less likely to clot inside the arteries and also improves cholesterol. It is an excellent source of B-vitamins, Niacin and B-12.*

In a medium pot, boil 4 cups water with juice of the lemons, placing one lemon half in the water. Reduce heat to a simmering boil. Poach salmon filet in water by cooking covered for 7 to 10 minutes, or until done. Remove with spatula. Set aside to cool. When salmon is cool, combine with celery, onions, mayonnaise, cayenne, tarragon, garlic, dry mustard, salt and black pepper in a large brown and mix well. Add dry potatoes slowly while mixing until everything is moist. Form patties and cook in preheated canola oil in a large skillet on medium high heat until both sides are brown.

*Nancy shares this special recipe for using fresh Salmon to be prepared into Salmon cakes. Simply prepared, yet a fabulous entrée.*

## Salmon Croquettes

1    (14 oz.) can pink salmon
1    large egg, lightly beaten
1/3  cup corneal mix
½    cup buttermilk
2    tbsp. self-rising flour
1/8  tsp. garlic salt
2    cups vegetable oil
Lemon-caper cream (see below)

Drain salmon; remove skin and bones and flake.  Place salmon in a medium bowl.  Stir in egg and next 4 ingredients until blended. (batter will be wet).  Drop salmon mixture by tablespoons into hot oil in a large skillet over medium-high heat, and slightly flatten with a fork.  Fry, in batches, 2 to 3 minutes on each side or until browned.  Drain on paper towels.  Keep warm on a wire rack in a jelly-roll pan in a 200 degree oven.  Serve with Lemon-Caper Cream.  Make Lemon-Caper Cream (1 cup): stir together ¾ cup light sour cream; 2 tbsp. capers, drained; 2 tbsp. mayonnaise; ½ tsp. lemon zest; and 1 tsp. lemon juice.  Season with salt and pepper to taste.  Store in air-tight container in refrigerator up to 2 weeks.

*Lemon caper sauce makes these salmon croquettes more appetizing tasty.*

> *Rolling on counter under the palm of your Hand and Heating a lemon briefly in the microwave will produce more juice.*

# Salmon, Seattle Style

Take piece of boneless, skinless salmon filet and coat lightly with olive oil.  Place in plastic storage bag along with sufficient Rub (see recipe below) to liberally coat.  Shake in bag until well covered.  Let sit in bag for ½ hour at room temperature.  Prepare cedar baking plank by oiling top of plank with olive oil, then place in oven middle rack and preheat oven to 370  degrees.  When preheat is complete, place salmon filet on plank and cook for 10-12 minutes (depending on thickness of filet) on first side then turn over.  Cook for 8-10 minutes on second side, open oven and pour ½ honey lime glaze (see recipe below) over salmon.  Turn on broiler leave temperature at 370 degrees and broil for 2 minutes to glaze.  Take out of oven and let sit for five minutes.

   Serve over yellow rice (preferably cooked in chicken broth rather than water, 1 tablespoon of butter and add 2-3 pieces of saffron to vigo brand yellow rice)  Provide remaining ½ of honey lime glaze, add to fish to taste.

   Salmon Rub:  ½ pound dark brown sugar, 1 and ½ tbsps. Cumin, 2 tbsps. Stubbs Chili Lime Rub (available at Target Superstore or Online), Substitute dark chili powder if unable to find above, 2 tbsp. lime pepper, Zest from 2 limes (reserve juice for glaze), 2 tbsp. Kosher Salt, 2 tbsp. of cilantro.  Combine all dry ingredients in quart freezer bag.  Shake will and crush together to combine well.  Makes sufficient for several salmon
servings.

   Salmon Glaze:  Juice from 2 limes, 4 ounces of honey, combine in microwaveable bowl, stir will then heat for about 20-3- seconds in microwave on high to combine.  Use ½ to glaze salmon while cooking and reserve ½ to provide as an accompaniment at serving time.  Makes enough for whole salmon filet.  Reduce according to portion prepared or save remainder in refrigerator for future use.  Also excellent on grilled chicken or broiled shrimp.

*Another good recipe from Trey Alley.  This is definitely a two-thumbs up delicious  salmon dish.  It will give you great raves when served.*

## Sausage Balls

1   box of Bisquick (smaller box 40oz)
1   8 oz. bag of sharp cheese
1   8 oz.  bag of medium cheese
1   roll of mild sausage
1   tube of hot sausage

Preheat oven to 350 degrees.  Start with half the box of Bisquick. Mix in the cheese and sausage. Add Bisquick as needed. You
don't want it to be too dry.  Roll into balls and place on ungreased
pan with edges. Cook for about 10-12 minutes or until firm.  Place on
paper towels to soak up grease from sausage.  Makes 1 batch which is
around 85-90 balls.


*Damaris is sharing one of her mother's recipe that has been used
for as long as she can remember.  She made them every Christmas
and for all the  wedding receptions.  Demaris and her daughter,
Kourtni,  still make them at Christmas and always have happy
memories when preparing this recipe.*

## Scalloped Oysters

1    pint oysters with liquor
2    cups saltine cracker crumbs
½  cup butter, melted
¾  cup half and half
¼  cup oyster liquor
½  tsp. Worcestershire  sauce
 Salt and pepper to taste

       Drain oysters, reserving liquor. Mix cracker crumbs with melted butter and place 1/3 in bottom of a greased baking dish. Cover with half the oysters.  Add another layer of cracker crumbs and place remaining oysters on top.  Make sauce by combining cream, oyster liquor, parsley, and Worcestershire sauce and season to taste with salt. Pour sauce over oysters and top with final layer of cracker crumbs.  Bake at 350 degrees in oven for 40 minutes.

Serves 4.


*This is another recipe furnished by Maggie's husband, Harold.  This is a very good dish and if you like oysters, you should give it a try.*

## <u>Scallops Newburg</u>

1   tbsp. garlic butter
1   lb. bay scallops, (thawed and drained if needed)
1   tsp. Old Bay Seafood Seasoning
1   (10.75 oz.) can condensed cream of shrimp soup
¼   cup sherry
1   (3 oz.) package cream cheese

Place garlic butter in large sauté pan on medium-high. Add scallops. Sprinkle with seafood seasoning. Cook 2 minutes, stirring occasionally, just until scallops are opaque. Stir in soup, sherry, and cream cheese until blended and smooth. Reduce heat to low. Cook 4-5 minutes or until thoroughly heated. Serve with rice or noodles.

*Scallops are quick-cooking and lend themselves to elegance in taste and presentation. This recipe can very nicely stand by itself as an appealing entrée.*

## Sesame Beef

1 lb. Flank steak or Flat iron steak - sliced very thin against the
     grain
1/2  cup soy sauce
2     tbsp. garlic, minced
2     tbsp. sesame oil
2     tsp. fresh ginger root, minced
1     tbsp. sugar
1     tbsp. rice wine vinegar
2     tbsp. sesame seeds
1     bunch scallions, sliced thin
1     tbsp. peanut oil
Salt & pepper to taste

      Marinade in a small bowl, whisk together soy sauce, garlic, sesame oil, minced ginger root, sugar, vinegar, sesame seeds, salt & pepper.  In a large zip lock bag, combine the steak & marinade & refrigerate overnight.  In a large skillet, heat the peanut oil over medium high.  Add marinated steak and scallions.  Cook, stirring occasionally until cooked through.   Sesame beef can be served over steamed rice.

*This superb dish, with a blaze of taste and simply prepared, is a fabulous entrée.  It's a good way to cook this cut of meat so that it will be tender.  Do not forget to slice against the grain.*

## Shrimp Casserole

1 ½   cups uncooked long-grain rice
1 ½   lbs.  raw shrimp
½      cup butter
1       green pepper, chopped
1       onion, chopped
3       celery ribs
4       green onions
2       cans cream of shrimp soup or celery soup
¼      tsp. salt
1       cup shredded  cheddar cheese
¼      cup fine, dry bread crumbs.

    Cook rice according to directions.  Peel shrimp and devein. Melt butter in large skillet.  Add bell pepper and next 4 ingredients. Sauté 10 to 12 minutes until tender.  Stir in soup, shrimp, salt and cook 3 minutes until shrimp turn pink.  Combine  rice with shrimp mixture and pour in 9 x 13 baking dish.  Sprinkle evenly with shredded  cheese and breadcrumbs.  Bake 25 minutes at 350 degrees until cheese melts.

*This is a very popular dish and is good for those covered dish get-togethers.  It is easy to prepare and will show you off as a good cook.*

## Steak Tips with Mushroom Gravy

2       cups uncooked egg  noodles
1       lb.  top sirloin steak, cut into 3/4 –inch pieces
1       tbsp. butter
2       tbsp. finely chopped shallots
1       (8-ounce) package pre-sliced baby bella mushrooms
1       tsp. minced garlic
1       tbsp. low-sodium soy sauce
3       tbsps.  all-purpose flour
1 ½  cups fat-free beef  broth
½       tsp. black pepper
¼       tsp. salt
3       fresh thyme sprigs

    Cook noodles according to package directions, omitting salt and fat .  Drain.  While noodles cook, heat a large nonstick skillet over  medium-high heat.  Coat pan with cooking spray.  Add steak. Sauté 5 minutes, browning on all sides.  Remove from pan and cover.  For mushroom gravy, melt butter in pan over medium-high heat.  Add shallots and mushrooms.  Sauté 4 minutes.  Add garlic and sauté 30 seconds.  Stir in soy sauce.  Whisk flour with little water and stir into mushroom mixture.  Cook 1 minute, stirring constantly.  Gradually add broth, stirring constantly.  Add pepper, salt, and thyme sprigs.  Bring to a boil.  Cook 2 minutes or until thickened.  Return beef to pan and cook 1 minute or until thoroughly heated.  Discard thyme sprigs.

*Whether your week-end is packed with errands or simply a date with ESPN, this special dish served with a salad and breadsticks is a guaranteed winner.  You may want to make two as it goes fast and it can be popped into the freezer for later.*

## Stuffed Chicken

1   (9oz.) pkg. creamed (Stauffer) spinach, thawed
¾   cup grated Swiss cheese
1   lb. thin cutlet filet of chicken
    salt and pepper to taste
2   lbs. parmesan cheese
7   slices of bacon

      Combine spinach and Swiss and parmesan cheese in bowl. Sprinkle chicken with salt.  Place small amount of spinach mixture in each filet.  Wrap one slice of bacon around each filet after rolling the filet with spinach inside.  Place in baking dish that has been sprayed with cooking spray.  Bake at 450 degrees for 25 to 30 minutes.  Makes 4 servings.  This stuffed chicken breast has only 390 calories per serving.

*Delicious chicken recipe and very easy to prepare.  It is a perfect dish for a busy lady to impress her family.*

## Turkey, roasted

10  lb turkey
1   onion, peeled and quartered
2   stalks celery, cut
4   sprigs parsley
2   ounces butter, melted
Salt and pepper to taste

Wash and remove inner trimmings  for making gravy.   Season and place onion, celery and parsley inside turkey.  Truss turkey, if necessary, and brush with melted butter.  Preheat oven to 425 degrees.  Place turkey breast-side –down on rack in roasting pan.  Bake for 30 min., basting once after 15 min.  Turn turkey breast-side-up and reduce oven temperature to 325 degrees.  Continue roasting and basting with pan juices every 15 to 20 minutes.  Roast approximately 15 to 20 minutes per pound or until meat thermometer registers 170 degrees.  Remove to warm platter.  Cover loosely with foil until ready to carve.  Make gravy from defatted pan drippings and cooked trimmings.

*This is a very good way to cook a turkey.  You will find you'll have a very tender, juicy meat.  A  turkey that is roasted without being stuffed lends to the excitement of trying totally different dressings on the side.*

> *The recipe below was written by Olivia, a student at Lake Oconee Academy, for the first grade "Thanksgiving Recipes" book. It was shared with our group and we wanted to pass it on for your consideration for your turkey dinner.*

## Turkey Dinner

8   pounds of rice
20  pounds of chicken
2   cups of broccoli
11  rolls
A   one-pound Turkey
2   cups celery
3   cups of chicken noodle soup

You need some rice and chicken to cook it. Let it cool off. Start cooking the chicken noodle soup. Set it down and go get some turkey. Buy some celery and get some chicken while you are at it. Cook it at the house.

*How precious it is to share the mind of a child. It is so amazing the joy we can receive when we allow them to expound their creative imagination. Thanks to the Lake Oconee Academy for allowing us to share some of the First Graders' cooking knowledge for Thanksgiving dishes.*

## Tuna Bake

1   cup macaroni (cooked 7 minutes)
3   oz. cream cheese ( softened)
1   can cream of mushroom soup
1   7 oz. can tuna drained and flaked
1 ½ tbsp. chopped pimentos, 1 T. chopped onions
1   tbsp.  prepared mustard
¼   cup milk
½   cup dry bread crumbs
2   tbsps.  melted butter

Blend softened cream cheese with  mushroom soup.  Stir in tuna, ½ tbsp. chopped pimentos, 1 tbsp. chopped onions, 1 tbsp. prepared mustard and ¼ cup milk.  Mix all together and add cooked and drained macaroni.  Top with ½ cup dry bread crumbs and 2 tbsp.  melted butter sprinkled over the top.  Bake at 375 degrees for 25 minutes.

*This is a favorite recipe of Beth MacKenney, Nancy's mother. Nancy has prepared this dish often for her family.  Grandma was always given the credit.*

# White Bean and Chicken Chili

2    tbsp.  olive oil
1    large onion, chopped
4    garlic cloves, minced
2    lb. ground chicken or ground turkey
1    tsp. salt, plus more for seasoning
2    tbsp. ground cumin
1    tbsp. fennel seeds
1    tbsp. dried oregano
2    tsp.  chili powder
3    tbsp.  flour
2 (15-ounce cans) white beans, rinsed and drained
1  bunch (1 pound) Swiss chard, chopped with stems removed
1 ½  cups frozen corn, thawed
4    cups low-sodium chicken stock
¼    teaspoon crushed red pepper flakes
1/2    cup grated Parmesan cheese
1/4    cup chopped fresh flat-leaf parsley
Freshly ground black pepper for seasoning

> *Doris felt this was a must for our cook-book.  The recipe calls for a lot of spices, but spices and seasonings help make healthy, low calorie meals that taste delicious.*

     In a large heavy-bottomed saucepan or Dutch oven, heat the oil over medium-high heat. Add the onion and cook until translucent, about 5 minutes. Add the garlic and cook for 30 seconds. Add the ground chicken, 1 teaspoon salt, cumin, fennel seeds, oregano, and chili powder. Cook, stirring frequently, until the chicken is cooked through, about 8 minutes. Stir the flour into the chicken mixture. Add the beans, Swiss chard, corn, and chicken stock. Bring the mixture to a simmer, scraping up the brown bits that cling to the bottom of the pan with a wooden spoon. Simmer for 55-60 minutes until the liquid has reduced by about half and the chili has thickened. Add the red pepper flakes and simmer for another 10 minutes. Season with salt and pepper, to taste.

Ladle the chili into serving bowls. Sprinkle with the Parmesan cheese and chopped parsley.  Serve with cheddar and scallion bread.  Recipe in Breads.

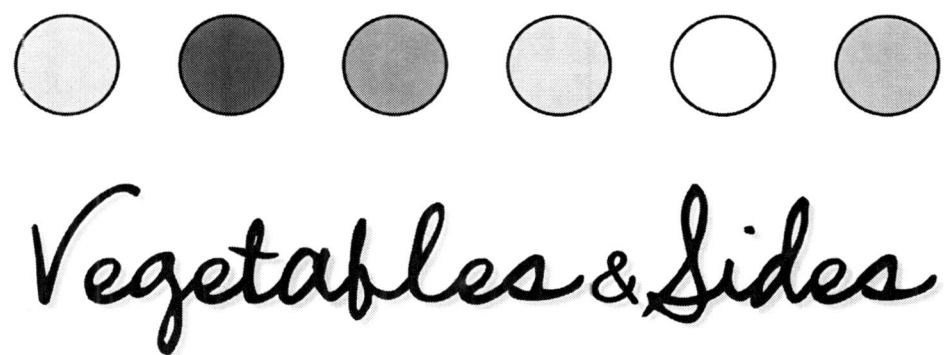

# Vegetables & Sides

There should always be one or two varieties of vegetables to accompany an entrée. Often, there would be more when a hospitable home was open for a Sunday dinner, and family members and friends would be invited to "come over for dinner" when church services were over. Such a spread of food would include Fried Chicken, Meats, Rice, Potato Salad, Stuffing, Sweet Potato Souffle and several fresh Vegetables fresh from the gardens accompanied by homemade Biscuits and Desserts.

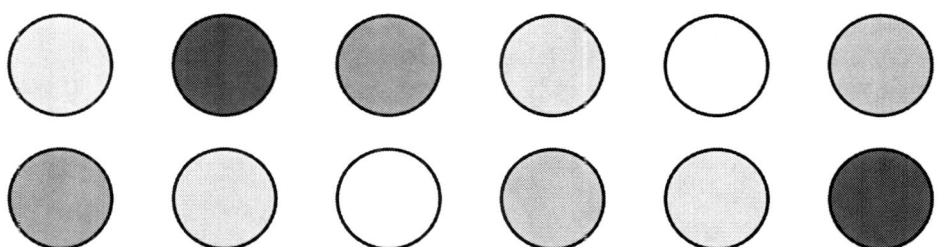

## Baked Macaroni and Cheese

½  pound 2 ½ inch elbow macaroni
1  small onion
¾  tsp. salt & pepper to taste
2  tbsp. butter or margarine
2  cups milk
1  tbsp. flour
½  lb. Velveeta cheese
¼  tsp. dried mustard
¾  cup bread crumbs
4  tsp. Melted butter

Cook macaroni.  Preheat oven to 400 degrees.  Grease 1 ½ quart casserole dish.  Mince onion and combine with 2 tbsp and when melted add flour, mustard, salt and pepper.  Slowly stir in milk.  Cook until smooth and hot.  Stir often.  Slice ¾ of cheese into sauce, and stir until cheese is melted.  Drain macaroni and pour into baking dish.  Combine cheese sauce, and toss with fork until macaroni gets coated.  Top with remaining cheese.  Toss bread crumbs with 4 tsp. of melted butter and sprinkle over cheese.  Pre-heat oven to 350 degrees and bake uncovered for 20 minutes at 350 degrees.

*Amy has wonderful memories of her mother's delicious dish of 'macaroni and cheese.  It was always a favorite for the family because they knew mom had put her heart into it.*

## Baked Ziti

1   box Rotatelle (spiral) macaroni
1   large jar Prego
1   8 oz. Ricotta cheese
1   8 oz. Mozzarella cheese- shredded
Parmesan cheese- grated

Line pan with sauce.  Put in cooked and drained maca-
roni.  Layer with ricotta cheese then  layer with mozzarella.  Sprinkle
with parmesan.  Put another layer of sauce, mozzarella, and parmesan.  Cover with foil.  Bake at 350 degrees for 30 minutes.  Uncover
last 5 minutes.

*Damaris was treated to this dish by her friend, Mallette.  It was so
good, she had to have the recipe and now is sharing it with everyone.   Her view of this dish was "wonderful".  We hope you will
agree.*

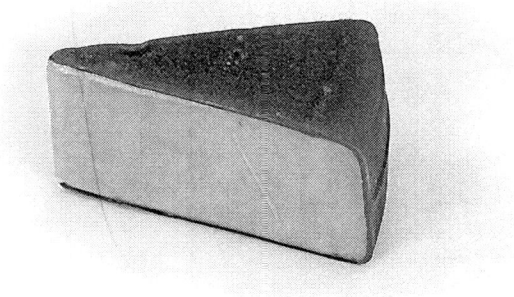

## Breakfast Casserole

5     slices of white or wheat bread.
1 ½ cups milk (turns out best if 1% or 2% is used…not skim)
6     eggs (beaten)
1     lb. browned and drained breakfast sausage
1     cup shredded cheddar cheese

    Use a greased (PAM works great) 9x13 glass dish.  Cut the slices of bread long ways into about 3 pieces per slice.  Lay them in the dish (you want them to be crowded in the pan as you should not see the bottom of the pan).  Spread the cooked sausage evenly over the bread.  Mix the milk and beaten eggs in a bowl and pour mixture over the sausage and bread.  Top with shredded cheese.  You can refrigerate overnight (works best), or you can cook immediately.  Bake at 400 degrees for about 30-45 minutes (It should look fluffy and golden brown on top when done).  Let it cool for about 5-10 minutes before serving

*This recipe is April's favorite.  It is an especially good dish to serve when having company.  It can be prepared the night before and then just popped in the oven in the morning.  Great for a family breakfast with a quick cleanup!*

## Broccoli Casserole

2   bunches of broccoli  (cook and drain)
1   lb. Velveeta cheese
2   tbsp. flour
2   cups milk
2   tbsp. butter
1   tsp. Worcestershire sauce
4   strips of bacon (cook and crumble)
Dash cayenne pepper

Cook washed fresh broccoli adding salt to taste.  Make sauce by melting butter slowly, add milk and whisk in flour.  Cook until thick,  then add Velveeta cheese and stir until melted.  Add Worcestershire sauce and dash of cayenne pepper.   Put cooked broccoli in bottom of dish,  add cheese and sauce mixture, then crumble cooked bacon over top.  Cook @ 350 degrees until it bubbles, about 15 min.

*Maggie is pleased to share this an outstanding recipe given to her by her granddaughter, Kristen.  It is delicious, easy to prepare, and a good way to make broccoli more appealing.*

## Broccoli Casserole 2

3    pkg. frozen broccoli or 1 large bunch fresh broccoli
1    can   mushroom soup
1    cup   grated cheese
½   cup mayonnaise
2    eggs, well beaten

        Cook broccoli (frozen or fresh) for 5 minutes or until tender.
Drain well.  Chop broccoli into small pieces.  Fold in the remaining
ingredients.  Put in buttered casserole dish.  Sprinkle top with
crushed Ritz crackers.  Dot with butter and bake at 350 degrees for
30 to 35 minutes.

*Shannon shares her favorite broccoli recipe.  It is one of those quick
dishes she can  put on the table in no time.  It fits in well with her
busy schedule.*

## Carrots, Ginger Glazed

1   (16 oz.) baby carrots
¾   cup water
2   tbsp. butter
¼   cup honey
1   tbsp. Orange juice
1   tsp. ground ginger
1/8  tsp.  salt
1/8  tsp.  nutmeg
½   tsp. parsley flakes

In a large skillet combine carrots, water and 1 tbsp. butter. Bring to boiling.  Reduce heat to medium.  Cover and cook for 8 minutes or until nearly tender.  In a small bowl combine honey, orange juice, ginger, salt, and nutmeg.  Pour over the carrots.  Add remaining butter.  Cook uncovered for about 6-8 minutes until tender, stirring frequently to glaze carrots.  Just before serving, sprinkle with parsley.

*Karen says this is a must for all carrot lovers.  It makes a very appealing dish and is very good for our health.  Take care of those eyes.*

## Cauliflower Gratin With Almond Crust

¼   cup butter
1    head cauliflower (about 2 ¼  lb.), separated into florets
1    small onion, chopped
2    garlic cloves, minced
2    tbsp. all-purpose flour
2    tsp. chopped fresh thyme
½    tsp. salt
½    cup whipping cream
1    cup (4 oz.) shredded Gruyere cheese
2/3  cup Japanese breadcrumbs (panko)
¼    cup sliced almonds
¼    cup grated Parmesan cheese

Preheat oven to 400 degrees.  Melt butter in a large skillet over medium-high heat.  Add cauliflower and next 2 ingredients. Sauté 10 minutes or until golden and just tender.  Sprinkle with flour and next 2 ingredients.  Stir well.  Remove from heat.  Spoon cauliflower mixture into an 11 x 7-inch baking dish, and drizzle with cream.  Sprinkle with Gruyere cheese and next 3 ingredients.  Bake at 400 degrees for 18 to 20 minutes or until golden.

*This is definitely a two-thumbs up!  Delicious results.  Doris makes it often for special quests and  for get-together outings.*

## Creamed or Mashed Potatoes

7   med. potatoes
½  cup half & half
½  cup butter
1   tbsp. mayonnaise
Salt and pepper to taste
Parsley flakes (1 tbsp)

Peel and dice potatoes. Bring water to a boil, Add salt, pepper and potatoes. Boil until tender, about 20 minutes. Pour off water and add butter. Cream potatoes with masher or electric beater. If potatoes too stiff, add a little more butter and half and half.

*Every household has to have a good mashed potato recipe. We think you will enjoy this one. We all know from watching Paula Dean, butter makes any food good. Adding the half and half even makes it better.*

## Caleb's Mashed Potatoes

**L.O.A. Kids**
Lake Oconee Academy
Thanksgiving Recipes

1 bottle of salt
2 potatoes
1 scoop of pepper
4 cups of milk

Peel the potatoes. Put the potatoes in the stove. Bake for 6 minutes at 6 degrees. Take the potatoes out of the oven and mash them up. Stir the salt, pepper and milk with the potatoes. Eat them!

*We want to share another Mashed Potato recipe taken from the "First Grade Thanksgiving Recipes" of the Lake Oconee Academy. This one is from Caleb.*

## Four Bean Dish Casserole

8   slices bacon
2   large onions, cut in rings
¾  cup brown sugar
1   tsp. dry mustard
½  tsp. garlic powder
1   tsp. salt
½  cup vinegar
1   (15oz.) can lima beans, drained
1   (16oz.) can green beans, drained
1   (15oz.) can kidney beans, drained
1   (28oz.) can England style baked beans, undrained

      Brown bacon and cool.  Cook onions in bacon drippings and then add seasonings and vinegar.  Cook slowly for 20 minutes.  Add beans and bacon.  Bake uncovered in 3 qt. casserole for 1 hour.


Beans, beans and beans.  This recipe sounds a little more appetizing than the one on the next page.

**L.O.A. Kids**
Lake Oconee Academy
Thanksgiving Recipes

## Kyles' Green Beans

100 cans green beans

You get the white can opener thing and when you hear the "click" it opens the lids. Drop it out into the pot. Leave it on the stove. If you see white smoke, don't leave it on the stove. Get it in a bowl, get a plate, and take it to my house. Yummy!

*Kyles is a first grade student at Lake Oconee Academy and this is his recipe for their Thanksgiving.*

## Hash Brown Casserole

I    bag of thawed shredded hash browns
1    (10) oz. can of cream of chicken soup (can use mushroom)
16  oz. sour cream
3    cups grated sharp cheddar cheese
1 ½  sticks of melted butter (separated)
3-4  cups of corn flakes (crushed)
Hot sauce (4-6 shakes)
Red pepper (if desired)

      Mix hash browns, soup, sour cream, cheese, hot sauce, red pepper, and 1 stick melted butter all together in a greased 9x13 glass dish. Mix corn flakes and ½ stick of butter together and spread evenly on top of hash brown mixture. Bake at 350 degrees for 1 hour.

*This is one of April's favorite recipes EVER. This casserole is good for Sunday brunch with fresh fruit salad and good home-made hot biscuits.*

## Hoppin John

1    lb. dried black-eyed peas (soaked about 2 hours)
1    cup chopped celery
1    medium bell pepper, chopped
2    medium onions, chopped
¾   lb. hog jowl, chopped fine (may use ham hocks or neck bones)

Combine all ingredients in pot and cook with plenty of water until done. Serve over rice.  May desire pepper sauce at table.

*No true Southerner omits this dish on New Years day.  The meal consists of black-eyed peas, hog jowl, greens, a big pot of rice and cornbread.  The peas were eaten for luck, jowl was eaten for health and the greens  were eaten for financial success.  This is a tradition passed down from generation to generation.*

## Italian Style Baked Beans

6    oz. thinly sliced pancetta, chopped
2    onions, chopped
4    garlic cloves, minced
1    cup dark beer
1    cup tomato sauce
1/3  cup dark brown sugar
1/4  cup balsamic vinegar
3    tbsp. mild-flavored molasses
6    tsp. Dijon mustard
3/4 tsp. salt
½    tsp. freshly ground black pepper
4    (15-ounce) cans cannellini beans, drained

Preheat the oven to 400 degrees F.  Cook the pancetta in a heavy large oven-safe pot over medium heat until crisp, about 8 minutes. Add the onions and garlic, and sauté until the onions are translucent, about 5 minutes.   Mix in the beer, tomato sauce, brown sugar, vinegar, molasses, mustard, salt, and pepper.  Stir in the beans. Bring to a simmer.  Transfer to the oven and bake, uncovered, until the bean mixture bubbles and thickens slightly, stirring occasionally, about 45 minutes.

*Doris says this is a winner every time.   All the ingredients enhance the beans.  A must try.*

## Marinated Carrots

2   lb.  carrots, sliced
1   can tomato soup
1   onion, diced
1   green pepper, diced
¼  cup oil
1   cup sugar
Dash of Worcestershire sauce

      Mix together tomato soup, onion, green pepper, oil, sugar, and Worcestershire sauce for marinade.  Add carrots and marinate overnight.  Bake at 350 degree for 45 minutes or until bubbling.

*Maggie's mother prepared this often and told  her family if they ate a lot of carrots, they would always have good eyesight.  Another old adage: does it work?  Who knows.*

## Ms. Sandra's Baked Beans

| | |
|---|---|
| 2 | cans 28 oz. Bush's home-style baked beans |
| 1 | can kidney beans, drained |
| 1 | can butter beans, drained |
| 3/4 | lb. bacon, cooked |
| 3/4 | lb. ground beef, browned |
| 1/2 | cup vinegar |
| 1/2 | c up brown sugar |
| 1/2 | cup onion, chopped |
| 8 | oz. molasses |
| 1 | tsp. mustard |

Brown ground beef and drain off all grease. Fry Bacon and break into small pieces. Mix all of the ingredients together; cover & bake at 350° for an hour. Remove cover and bake for another 30 minutes or so. Stir often.

*DeAnn and her family think this is a delicious alternative to traditional baked beans and they have been enjoying it for a long time. Great for an outdoor cookout.*

## One Pot Creamy Pasta

4   large garlic cloves, peeled
1   jar, (7 oz.) sun-dried tomatoes in oil, undrained
3   cans (14.5 oz each) chicken broth (5 ¼ cups)
1   lb. uncooked penne pasta
1   head broccoli, (2 cups small florets)
2   medium carrots, peeled
4   oz. reduce-fat cream cheese
¼   tsp.  salt
½   tsp.  black pepper
   Grated fresh parmesan cheese
   Snipped fresh basil (optional)

> *Audrey says this is a good choice for a week-night complete meal and the kids love it. Great served with a salad and crusty French bread.*

Thinly slice garlic. Place garlic and 1 tbsp. oil from sun-dried tomatoes into 8 qt. pot.  Cook garlic until golden brown, stirring occasionally. Remove from heat; add broth.  Cover and bring to boil on high.  Stir in pasta; cover and simmer vigorously 8-10 minutes or until pasta is almost cooked but still firm, stirring occasionally.

Meanwhile, cut broccoli into small florets. Cut carrots in half lengthwise.  Drain sun-dried tomatoes; pat dry with a paper towel. Slice tomatoes into thin strips.

Cut cream cheese into cubes. Add vegetables, cream cheese, salt and pepper to pot.  Stir until cream cheese is melted and fully mixed. Reduce heat to medium; cover and cook and additional 2-4 minutes or until vegetables are tender. Serve immediately. If desired top with grated fresh Parmesan cheese and snipped fresh basil. Makes 6-8 servings.

For a heartier version add grilled turkey, Italian sausage or slice grilled chicken breast to pasta.  If desired, 2 cups halved cherry tomatoes can be substituted for the sun-dried tomatoes.

## Orange Sweet Potatoes

| | |
|---|---|
| 8 | med. sweet potatoes (about 4 pounds) |
| ½ | cup packed brown sugar |
| 4 | tbsp.  cornstarch |
| ½ | tsp. salt |
| ½ | tsp. ground cinnamon |
| 1 | cup  orange juice |
| 3 | tbsp. butter |
| 2 | tbsp. water |
| 2 | tbsp. grated orange peal |
| ½ | cup walnuts |

Place sweet potatoes in soup kettle and cover with water. Bring to boil.  Reduce heat, cover, and simmer for 25-30 minutes or until tender.  Drain.  When cool, peel and cut into ½ inch slices.  Arrange in greased shallow 3 quart baking dish.  Set aside.  In saucepan, combine brown sugar, cornstarch, salt, and cinnamon.  Stir in orange juice, honey, butter, water and orange peel.  Bring to boil, cook and stir for 2 minutes or until thickened.  Stir in the walnuts.  Pour the mixture over the potatoes.  Bake uncovered at 350 degrees for 25 minutes or until heated through.  Yields 12 servings.

*Tam has come up with a good sweet potato dish.  It doesn't get much easier than this dish.  A few minutes in preparation and the oven does the rest.  The orange juice and peel gives this recipe some zip.*

## Pumpkin Sage Risotto or Butternut Squash

| | | |
|---|---|---|
| 2 | tbsp. | butter and 1 tbs. olive oil |
| 2 | | shallots, chopped |
| 1 | | clove garlic, chopped |
| ¼ | cup | chopped onions |
| 2 | cups | vegetable or chicken broth |
| 1 | cup | Arborio rice |
| ¼ | cup | red or white wine |
| ½ | cup | parmesan or goat cheese |
| 1 ½ | cups | pumpkin or butternut squash cubes |
| 2 | tbsp. | fresh chopped sage and salt, pepper to taste |

(This recipe can be made in pressure cooker 7 minutes or longer in a large pot)

Preheat oven to 400 degrees.  Place the pumpkin or squash in a bowl and season with salt and pepper.  Spray the vegetables with cooking spray.  Place in the oven and roast for 25 to 30 minutes. Meanwhile heat the butter and oil in the pressure cooker.  Add shallots, garlic and onions. Sauté for 2 minutes, stirring constantly. Add the rice and stir for 1 minute.  Add stock and wine, close and cook for 7 minutes in pressure cooker  or longer in a large pot.

*Nancy says no one thought this recipe would be good but her!  Now it is a favorite with her family.*

## Roasted  Acorn Squash

2     acorn or spaghetti squash, halved and seeded
2     tbsp.  butter, melted or olive oil if dieting
¼     tsp. salt
 Nutmeg to sprinkle

      Preheat the oven to 400 degrees.  Spray a pryex dish with nonstick spray.  Halve and halve again. Brush the flesh with melted butter or oil.   Then sprinkle with the salt, and place in pryex dish flesh side down.  Cover with foil and roast 30 minutes.  Uncover and roast 30 minutes or until lightly browned and very soft.  Then sprinkle with nutmeg.

*Maggie was given this recipe by the chef at the Southern Cross Horse Ranch near Madison, Ga.   This is an outstanding restaurant and the food is so well prepared as well as delicious.  This is a very good way to prepare squash.*

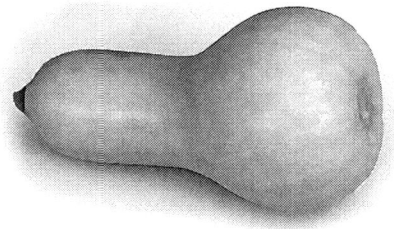

## Roasted Turnips With Honey Butter

3    tbsp. butter
3    tbsp. honey
2    lb. turnips, peeled and cubed
1    tsp. salt
½    tsp. pepper
¼    cup chopped fresh parsley

Preheat oven to 400 degrees. Place butter and honey in a glass measuring cup. Microwave at HIGH 45 seconds or until melted. Stir until blended. Place turnips on an aluminum foil-lined baking sheet. Sprinkle with salt and pepper. Drizzle with butter mixture, tossing to coat. Bake at 400 degrees for 30 to 35 minutes or until golden brown. Transfer turnips to a serving bowl. Pour any accumulated liquid over turnips. Toss turnips with parsley.

*Tam shares this very old and tried recip. It is a great way to cook turnips.*

## Savannah Red Rice

2   cups rice (cooked)
2   medium bell peppers
2   medium onions
4   strips bacon (fried crisp)
1   can tomatoes
1   cup tomato sauce or catsup
½ Tabasco Sauce
1   tsp. Parmesan Cheese
Salt and pepper to taste

    Fry bacon, remove and place on paper towel.  Brown onion and bell pepper in drippings.  Add tomatoes, sauce, Tabasco and crumbled bacon.  Pour in greased casserole, sprinkle top with Parmesan cheese and bake at 325 for 30 minutes or until rice is dry enough to separate.

*This is a favorite recipe from Mrs. Wilkes Boarding House in Savannah, Ga.  Mrs. Wilkes graciously shared this with Maggie many years ago.  She made her living by being an excellent cook. She has been called the "Julia Child of country cooking".  To be able to eat in her restaurant, you have to stand in line for an hour or two.  No reservations, just first come, first served.  Her restaurant is now "World Renown".*

## Spaghetti Squash with Marinara

1    medium spaghetti squash
2    cups chopped tomatoes
1    cup sliced, fresh mushrooms
1    cup diced green pepper
½   cup shredded carrots
¼   cup red onion, chopped
2    garlic clove, minced
2    tsp. Italian seasoning
1/8  tsp. pepper
1    tbsp.  olive oil
1    can (15oz.) tomato sauce
Grated parmesan cheese

    Cut squash in half length wise, discard seeds.  Place squash
with cut side down on a dish or glass casserole dish and put ¼ cup
water in dish.  Cover with saran wrap and microwave on high 14-16
minutes or until tender (about 18-20 min.), and let cool.  Meanwhile,
in a large skillet sauté the tomatoes, mushrooms, green peppers, carrots, onion, garlic, Italian seasoning and pepper in oil for 6-8 minutes or until tender.  Add tomato sauce and heat through.  When
squash is cool enough to handle, use a fork to separate strands by
scrapping with the fork.  Place squash in a serving platter and top
with sauce.  Sprinkle with parmesan cheese.  Add meat if desired.


*Doesn't this dish sound delicious?  Another one of Nancy's favorites.*

## Spinach Casserole

| | |
|---|---|
| 1 | 10 oz.pkg frozen chopped spinach, thawed |
| 2 | tbsp. butter |
| 1 | med. onion (chopped, about ¾ cups) |
| 2 | garlic cloves, minced |
| 3 | large eggs |
| 2 | tbsp. all-purpose flour |
| ½ | tsp. salt |
| ¼ | tsp. nutmeg |
| 1 | cup milk |
| 1 | cup grated parmesan cheese |

Drain spinach, press between paper towel, removing all liquid. Melt butter in skillet. Add onion and garlic until lightly browned. Stir in spinach until well blended. Cool. Whisk eggs and next 4 ingredients, then whisk in milk and cheese. Stir in spinach mixture. Bake at 350
degrees for 30 to 35 min.

*Something quick and easy to put together for last minute company and family get-togethers. A good way to get the young ones to eat spinach.*

## Squash Casserole

| | |
|---|---|
| 2 ½ | lbs. yellow squash |
| ½ | cup butter |
| 1 | cup sour cream |
| 1 | (10 ¾ oz.) cream of chicken soup (undiluted) |
| 2 | onions chopped |
| 1 5 | oz. can water chestnuts, drained |
| 1 2 | oz. jar pimento, drained |
| 8oz. | herb seasoned stuffed dressing mix |

Cook squash in boiling water until tender, reserving 1 ½ cups liquid. Season to taste with salt and pepper. Combine reserved liquid to remaining ingredients except ½ cup stuff mix. Stir in squash. Pour mixture into a 2 ½ quart casserole. Top with reserved stuff mix. Bake for 30 minutes at 350 degrees.

*Maggie shares this recipe which is a favorite with her family. They still request it when they plan a visit and are hungry for a good home cooked meal.*

## Squash Casserole #2

7    crookneck squash (cooked)
1    medium onion
2    grated carrots
1    cup lite sour cream
1    can cream of chicken soup
½    stick of butter
2    cups stuffing mix
Salt and pepper

     Melt butter in pan and pour 1 cup stuffing mix on top.  Mix all other ingredients together and put in dish.  Top with rest of stuffing. Bake at 350 degrees for 30 minutes.

*This is an old standby with Nancy.  She has been preparing this dish since early marriage days.  A squash casserole was always found on the table at her Mom's house.*

## Summer Vegetable Skillet

| | |
|---|---|
| 1 | med. zucchini |
| 1 | med. yellow squash |
| ½ | lb. fresh okra |
| ½ | lb. peeled potatoes |
| 1 | cup Jiffy cornmeal |
| 1 | tsp. salt |
| 1 | tsp. ground red pepper |
| 4 | bacon slices (cooked) |
| ½ | cup vegetable oil |

Cut zucchini, squash, okra and potatoes into 1 inch cubes. Combine cornmeal, salt and red pepper in a large heavy-duty zip-top plastic bag. Add veggies, seal and shake to coat. Cook bacon until crispy and crumble. Add oil to skillet and place over medium high heat until hot. Add half of veggie mixture, and cook over high heat stirring often for 15 minutes. Cover and reduce heat to low for 15 minutes more. Remove from skillet, and keep warm. Repeat with remaining veggie mixture. Sprinkle with bacon.

*Nancy says this is a great recipe for preparing those fresh summer vegetables. It may take a little of your time but it is well worth it.*

## Sweet Corn Pudding

| | |
|---|---|
| 1 | cup fresh breadcrumbs |
| 6 | tbsp. self-rising white cornbread mix |
| 1 ½ | tbsp. sugar |
| 1 | tsp. salt  3  large eggs |
| 1 ¼ | cup milk |
| ½ | cup half and half |
| 1 | (20 oz.) pkg. frozen cream-style corn, thawed |
| 2 | tbsp. butter |

Combine first 4 ingredients in large bowl. Whisk eggs until pale and foamy. Then whisk in milk, half and half, and butter. Then whisk into bread crumbs mixture. Stir in corn. Pour into lightly greased 9 inch square baking dish. Bake at 325 degrees for 60 minutes to 65 minutes until set. Let stand 10 minutes.

*This recipe goes a long way back. It has been passed around a lot of times. It goes over well with the family. We hope you enjoy.*

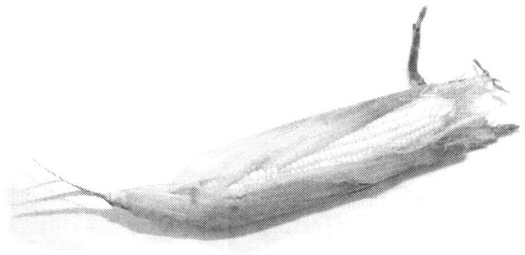

## Sweet Potato Casserole

3 cups mashed sweet potatoes (3 lbs. fresh, boiled)
½ stick butter
1 can low-fat eagle brand milk
1/3 cup sugar
2 eggs
½ tsp. cinnamon
½ tsp. nutmeg
½ tsp. vanilla

 Mix all ingredients thoroughly.  Place in buttered casserole dish and bake in preheated oven at 400 degrees for 30 minutes.

Topping
1 cup crushed corn flakes
½ cup brown sugar
½ stick butter
½ cup chopped pecans

 Mix this topping and spread on top of casserole.  Bake another 15 minutes at 400 degrees.

*Everyone loves sweet potato casseroles, and we found we had more good ones  than room to print all of them for you.  Hope we selected just the one you will think to be the "best".*

## Sweet Potato Casserole #2

4   cups sweet potatoes, cooked, peeled and mashed
1   cup sugar
2   eggs
1   tsp. vanilla
½   tsp. nutmeg, salt, and cinnamon
½   stick butter

Mix well and put in 9x13  inch glass lasagna pan.

Topping
1   cup coconut
1/3  cup self-rising flour
1   cup brown sugar
½ stick butter
1   cup chopped nuts

Mix well until it resembles crumb topping. Cover potatoes with the topping and bake at 350 degrees for 35 minutes.

*Barbara has been making this dish for her family for many years. Southerners often speak reverently when discussing sweet potato casseroles.6  No holiday table should be without it.*

## Sweet Potato Soufflé

Soufflé
3     cup sweet potatoes, baked and mashed
1     cup sugar
½     tsp.salt
2     eggs, lightly beaten
1/3     stick butter, melted
½     cup milk
1     tsp. vanilla
1     tsp. cinnamon
Topping
1/3     stick butter
1     cup brown sugar
1/3     cup flour
1     cup chopped pecans

Preheat oven to 350°. Mix all soufflé ingredients together and pour into greased baking dish. Mix all topping ingredients together and cover soufflé with nut topping. Bake 35 minutes.

*This recipe has been in Maggie's family for many years. Her mother always made it for family gatherings and took it to many church suppers. Easy to make and delicious to eat.*

## Tomato Pie

1   pie shell
4   fresh tomatoes, sliced
1   cup Mayo
1   cup shredded Cheddar cheese
1   cup shredded Mozzarella cheese
½ cup  green onions, chopped
Fresh basil, chopped
Salt and pepper to taste

     Put pie shell in 9 inch pie plate and bake for 10 minutes at 350 degrees.  Mix cheese's and mayo together.  In pie shell layer onions, basil, sliced tomatoes, and salt and pepper.  Spread ½ of the cheese and mayo mixture.  Repeat layers and top with sliced tomatoes.  Bake at 350 degrees for 30-45 minutes (cheese should be melted good).

*Karen says this is a very enjoyable dish.  People rave every time that she serves it.  It is especially good when Vidalia Onions are in season and substituted for the green onions.  Hope you enjoy.*

*Lewis Grizzard always said, "It's difficult to think anything but pleasant thoughts while eating a home grown tomato".  We agree.*

## Tortilla Pie

1    (16 oz.) can refried beans
1    tsp. chili powder
½   tsp. ground cumin
8    (8 inch) flour tortillas
½   (16 oz.) jar chunky salsa
2    (4 oz.) cartons guacamole
1    (8oz.) package shredded Mexican cheese blend
Garnish: fresh cilantro sprig, sour cream

Combine first 3 ingredients in a small bowl, stirring well, and set aside.  Place 1 tortilla in a lightly greased 9 inch round cake pan.  Spread with half of bean mixture, and top with another tortilla.  Spread with half of salsa and top with another tortilla.  Spread with half of guacamole and top with another tortilla.  Sprinkle with half of shredded cheese and top with another tortilla.  Repeat layers with remaining ingredients, ending with cheese.  Cover with foil.  Bake at 350 degrees for 20 minutes or until thoroughly heated.  Cut pie into wedges.  Garnish if desired.  Yields 6 servings.


 *Nancy feels this recipe deserved a spot in our recipe book.  It's easy to make and is very good.  She gets lots of requests  to make this dish.*

## Uncle Joe's Baked Beans

8    slices bacon, cut into 1/2 –inch pieces
1    onion, chopped
1    can (12 ounces) Coca-Cola
1    tbsp. Dijon mustard
1    tsp.  hot pepper sauce
1    can (15 ounces) kidney beans, drained
1    can (15 ounces) pinto beans, drained
2    cans (8 ounces each) crushed pineapple, drained

      Cook bacon and onion over medium-high heat in large skillet until bacon is browned and crispy.  Drain fat.  Set aside.  Preheat oven to 375 degrees.  Spray 13 x 9- inch casserole with nonstick cooking spray.

Meanwhile, combine Coca-Cola, tomato paste, mustard and hot pepper sauce in large bowl.  Mix well.  Add beans, pineapple and bacon mixture to Coca-Cola mixture.  Mix well.  Transfer to prepared dish. Bake uncovered for 20 to 25 minutes or until beans are hot and bubbly.  Makes 4 to 6 servings.

*Amy loves to prepare those recipes calling for our famous Georgia "Coca Cola".  She finds that everyone who has partaken of this dish, loves it.  Serve it at that next outdoor barbeque with family and friends.*

## Vidalia Onion Casserole

6    med. or large Vidalia onions, cut in chunks
3    tbsp. butter
1    cup cooked rice
1    cup grated Swiss cheese
2/3 cup milk or part Half and Half
½    tsp. salt

Sauté onions in butter in large skillet until golden and translucent, but not brown. Add rice, cheese, and milk. Pour into casserole. Bake 45 minutes at 325 degrees. Yields 4 servings. For one dish meal, chopped ham may be added.

*This is a great recipe when using the famous "Vidalia or Glennville Onions".*

## Vidalia Onion Pie

I     deep dish pastry shell
3     cups thinly sliced Vidalia onions or other sweet onions
3     tbsp. melted butter
½     cup milk
1½   cups sour cream
3     eggs, beaten
3     tbsp. flour
4     strips bacon, fried and crumbled

       Bake pastry shell. Cook onions in butter until lightly browned. Spoon into pastry shell. Combine milk, sour cream, salt, eggs and flour. Mix well and pour over onion mixture. Garnish with bacon. Bake at 325 degrees, 30 minutes or until firm in the center. Serves 6 to 8.

*This was the favorite of Maggie's late sister, Betty. She was not a great cook but she sure did know how to prepare the "Glennville and Vidalia Onions" and she did a good job with this dish.*

> *Life is an onion and one cries while pealing it.*

# Fed by Grace

# Desserts & Sweets

Desserts have always played an important part at the dining table. Sunday dinners of long ago always had a sideboard displaying cakes, pies, and puddings. Most popular of all time was and still is the Apple pie especially with most men. Banana Pudding, Pecan Pie and Homemade Ice Cream come to mind when thinking of other all time favorites. Recipes often began with words "take a quart of heavy whipping cream". We always had to have ambrosia which to this day is a traditional Thanksgiving and Christmas dessert in many homes. Some favorite recipes include Egg Custard Pies, Pecan Pies, Sweet Potato Pies, Lemon Pie and deep dish fruit pies using peaches, blackberries, blueberries or pears from the farm. Cakes always included everyone's favorite pound cake. We had many outstanding recipes submitted for this cookbook and we hope that the ones we have selected to use will become one of your favorite.

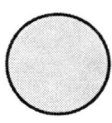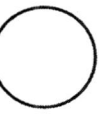

## Apple Crisp

5        apples
¾        cup maple syrup
½        tsp. nutmeg
¾        tsp. cinnamon
½        cup all-purpose flour
½        cup rolled oats
½        cup brown sugar
½        cup  butter
Pinch  Salt

Preheat oven to 375°.  Place apples in 8 x 8 baking dish.  Toss apples with syrup, nutmeg and cinnamon.  In a  separate bowl mix flour, oats, sugar and salt.  Cut in butter until crumbly.  Sprinkle over apples.  Bake 35 minutes.

*This is the "Easiest  Apple Crisp  ever".  This dish is quick and delicious.  Enjoy!  When you cook apples, it always makes your home smell good.  Enjoy!*

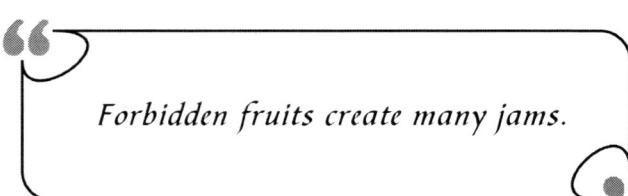

Forbidden fruits create many jams.

## Apple Dump Cake

2     cans or 4 cups of apples, cooked to desired texture
1     can crushed pineapple
1/2   box of brown sugar
1     box Dunkin Hines butter recipe cake mix
1     stick of butter

Spray a 9 x 13 pan with Pam. Spread the pineapple evenly to cover bottom of pan. Spread cake mix over pineapple. Then cover with the brown sugar. Cut butter into slices and cover the brown sugar. Bake at 350 degrees until golden brown and bubbling (45 minutes to an hour).

*Tam shares this recipe from a dear friend, Ms. Gwynn, whom she describes as a fine example of a southern woman. This tasty dish can be even better with a big scoop of vanilla ice cream.*

Fed by Grace

## Banana Pudding

½  cup sugar
½  cup splenda
3   tbsp. flour
3   egg yolks, beaten
1   tbsp. vanilla
2   cups half and half
5   bananas
20  vanilla  wafers
 Dash of salt

     Combine sugar, flour, and dash of salt.  In double boiler, mix egg yolks and vanilla.  Add sugar mixture.   Slowly add half and half, stirring often.  Cook until thick.  In a Pyrex baking dish, layer vanilla wafers and banana slices.  Pour above mixture over each layer.


*Maggie says this is by far the best  dessert that is served at Mrs. Wilkes Boarding House in Savannah.  It is especially good with  lots of meringue  topping. Mrs. Wilkes does not use splenda,  but Maggie  does, and feels it  is just as good without the calories. Eating here is  an eating experience you should enjoy when you visit the beautiful city of Savannah, Ga.  The atmosphere is warm, and it is fun to eat with others from all over the world.*

## Matt's Banana Pie

    14    bananas
    10    eggs
           pie shell
           whipped cream

     Peel bananas.  Put bananas in bowl with eggs.  Put into a pie shell and bake for 47 minutes at 100 degrees.  Put whipped cream on top.  Eat it.  How does this one sound?

*You may want to try Matt's Banana Pudding  recipe.  He is a  first grader at Lake Oconee Academy.   This is  one of the First Grade Thanksgiving recipes.*

## Bed & Breakfast Cookies

1   box cake mix (any kind, any brand)
2   eggs
½  cup peanut oil

     Take box cake mix and throw away the box. Mix together with eggs and oil. This is the cookie dough. Now, you may want to add some chocolate chips. If so, please use devil's food cake mix and add ½ cup of chips. If using spice or pecan cake mix, add pecans or white chocolate chips. Just use imagination. Bake cookies at 350 degree for 12 to 14 minutes. Do not overcook. Use cookie sheet with parchment paper. Enjoy.

*This recipe was given to Maggie many years ago by the chef of a Bed & Breakfast Inn in Savannah, Ga. This is a favorite with the young people.*

## Blueberry Pie

1   cup flour
1   stick of butter
½   cup sugar
1   cup chopped nuts

Make a cookie crust bottom by melting butter and combine all together and mix. Press in pan until it forms a thin layer on the bottom. Bake at 350 degrees until browned a little. Cool completely.

1   small carton cool whip
1/4 cup sugar
8   oz. cream cheese (room temp)

Make filling by blending cool whip, cream cheese, sugar together and blend until smooth. Pour over cooled crust. Refrigerate 1-2 hours or overnight.

Top with 1 can blueberry pie filling before serving (other pie filling flavors could be used). You can add another layer of cool whip over blueberries for a layered look.

*Nancy thinks this is a must try pie. It is something quick and easy to put together for company and family get-togethers.*

## Bread Pudding with Peaches, Cream and Amaretto Sauce

4   tbsp. unsalted butter, softened, (plus 4 tbsp. melted for top)
6   cups 1-inch cubes of day-old bread
2   cups heavy cream
2   cups milk
2   lbs. peaches, peeled and cut in chunks  (canned peaches may be
      used)
1   cup sugar
5   large eggs
1   tsp. pure vanilla extract
1/4 teaspoon freshly grated nutmeg

Preheat oven to 350.  Butter a large baking dish with 1 tbsp.  of the softened butter.  In large bowl, combine bread cubes, heavy cream and milk and let sit for 15 minutes, stirring often.  While bread soaking, heat remaining 3 tbsp. of butter in a large skillet. Then add peaches and 1/4 cup of the sugar.  Cook, stirring often, until peaches are golden and softened .  Set aside.  In a med. bowl, combine eggs, the remaining 3/4 cup sugar, vanilla, and nutmeg and whisk well. Stir the egg mixture into the bread mixture and fold to combine. Add the warm peaches and blend.  Pour into the prepared dish.  Drizzle with the 4 tbsp. melted butter and bake until golden brown and slightly firm, 45 minutes to 1 hour. Cool until just warm.

**Amaretto Sauce**:  In a small  saucepan over low heat, melt 1 stick of butter In a small bowl combine 1 cup heavy  cream, 1 cup sugar, and 2 egg yolks.  Add the cream mixture to the melted butter. Cook, stirring until  the sauce thickens.  Remove from heat and add amaretto.   Pour in dish and spread over pudding as desired.

*This is an outstanding  recipe from Doris. It's a decadent version of a Southern classic.  It is wonderful without the sauce, but why would you want to do that.  However, you could omit the amaretto and add a little vanilla for an alcohol free version.*

## Brownies

| | |
|---|---|
| 1 | cup butter |
| 2 | cup sugar |
| 3 | eggs |
| 1 | tsp. vanilla |
| 4 | oz. chocolate (12 tbsp cocoa) |
| 1 | cup self rising flour |

Preheat oven to 350°.  Cream butter and sugar together until light; add vanilla.  Sift together cocoa and flour; blend into butter mixture.  Pour into greased and floured 13x9 pan.  Bake about 45 minutes.

*DeAnn could be called the brownie cooking queen.  These brownies are everything a brownie should be, and are especially popular with the young ones.*

## Mariah's Chocolate Brownies

**L.O.A. Kids**
Lake Oconee Academy
Thanksgiving Recipes

2   things of chocolate
1   thing of bread
3   things of milk
4   cups of water

Put all ingredients in a bowl and mix them up.  Then you put them on a tray.  Then you put them in the oven.  Turn the oven on. Cook them for 10 minutes.  Take them out and eat them.  They are really good if you put chocolate syrup on top of them.

*Another favorite Brownie recipe we found in the Lake Oconee First Grade Thanksgiving Recipes given by Mariah.  Thought you may be interested!*

## Buttermilk Pie

| | |
|---|---|
| 3 | eggs |
| 1 | cup sugar |
| 3 | tbsp. flour (plus a little for dusting) |
| ½ | cup butter, melted |
| 1 | cup buttermilk |
| 1 | tsp. vanilla extract |
| 1 | 9 inch pie shell, unbaked |

Preheat oven to 325°. Beat eggs slightly; add eggs, sugar and flour. Then add melted butter and mix well. Add buttermilk and vanilla; mix thoroughly. Dust the unbaked pie shell with a bit of flour. Pour batter into shell and then sprinkle a little more flour on top. Bake until custard is set (about an hour).

*This is Deann's favorite recipe. She had a piece of buttermilk pie from a local restaurant and had to try to learn to make it. She ended up with an even better recipe, and it receives many accolades.*

## Caramel Crème Brulee

1  cup sugar (may substitute half with splenda)
5  eggs
2  cups milk
1  cup half and half
1/2  tsp. vanilla
Pinch of salt
Nutmeg (sprinkle on top)

For caramel sauce, melt ½ cup sugar until it becomes a light brown syrup, stirring constantly. Pour syrup into bottom of 8 custard cups that have been lightly sprayed with Pam or buttered. Place the custard cups in a large baking pan. Preheat oven to 350 degrees. In large bowl mix at low speed, eggs, salt, sugar until well blended. Gradually mix in milk, half and half and vanilla. After settled and bubbles out, pour mixture evenly into the cups. Pour hot water into baking pan to within 1 inch of top of cups. Bake for 1 hour or until knife inserted in center comes out clean. Cool. Run around edges with knife and then invert when served. About 3 tbsp. brandy sure enhances the taste.

*This is one of Maggie's favorite. She got the recipe from The Cloister in Sea Island many years ago. It is one of her most desired desserts. It is very easy to make once you can get the caramel sauce down pat. You may want to double the recipe for a dinner party of 8 or more.*

## Chewy Cake

1   lb.  dark brown sugar
1   stick butter
2   eggs
1   tsp.  vanilla
2   cups self-rising flour
2   cups chopped nuts

Mix all ingredients together (except nuts).  Mixture will be thick.  Add nuts and spread mixture over a greased 9 x 13 pan.  Bake in preheated oven 325 degrees for 30 minutes.  Cut in squares when cool.  Store in light container

*A good one made by Maggie's mother for many years.  You know it will be good because it has been tried and tested by many.  Everyone will love this treat.*

*The good Lord didn't create anything without a purpose, but mosquitoes come close.*

## Egg Custard Pie

| 1 | cup sugar (I use ½ cup splenda and ½ cup sugar) |
| 1/3 | cup butter |
| 2 | cups scalded milk |
| 4 | eggs |
| 1 | pinch salt |
| 1 | tsp vanilla |

Nutmeg to sprinkle on top

Deep dish pie crust (pre-cooked at 400 degrees 10 minutes). Cream butter (at room temperature) with sugar. Add salt, vanilla and then 1 egg at a time using electric mixer. Add milk. Then pour into prepared pie crust. Sprinkle nutmeg on top. Bake at 425 for 10 minutes and then reduce to 300 degrees for 20 minutes or until edges are firm and knife inserted in center comes out clean.

*This pie always comes out of the oven perfectly cooked. By using splenda (less calories) you can eat more. This is also one of the old dinner-on-the-ground favorites.*

*Don't let your worries get the best of you; remember, Moses started out as a basket case.*

## Lemon Cake

1     pkg. (2-layer size) yellow cake mix
2     cups cold milk
1 ¼ cups water
2   pkg. (4-serving size each) jello-lemon instant pudding and pie
     filling
1/3  cup granulated sugar
2    tsp. powdered sugar

     Preheat oven to 350 degrees and prepare cake mix as directed. Pour into greased 13x9 inch baking dish.  Pour milk and water into a large bowl.  Add dry pudding mixes and granulated sugar.  Beat with wine whisk for 2 minutes or until well blended.  Pour over cake batter in dish.  Place baking dish on baking sheet to catch runover.  Bake 55 minutes to 1 hour at 350 degrees or until toothpick inserted in center comes clean.  Cool in pan 20 minutes (will thin slightly as it cools).  Sprinkle with sugar (powdered).

*Barbara  shares this recipe that was handed down by her mother which was handed down by her mother, and grandmother.  It has been around for a long time.*

## Chocolate Dipped Butter Cookies

1      cup butter
½   cup sifted confectioner's sugar
1      tsp. vanilla extract
2      cups all purpose flour
16   oz.  chocolate chips
1      tbsp. shortening
½   cup finely chopped pecans

Preheat oven to 350 degrees.  Cream  butter, add sugar, beating it until it is light and fluffy.  Stir in vanilla and add flour.  Mix well.  Shape dough into 2 inches x 1 inch sticks on an ungreased but non-stick cookie sheet.  Flatten ¾ of each cookie with a fork to a ¼ inch thickness.  Bake at 350 degrees for 12-14 minutes.  Cool on wire rack.  Combine chocolate chips and shortening in the top of double boiler.  Cook until chocolate melts, stirring occasionally.  Leave chocolate over hot water.  Dip UNFLATTENED tips of cookie in chocolate; coat both sides.   Roll tips in chopped pecans.  Put on wire rack or wax paper to dry

*This recipe came from April's grandmother's best friend Ruth.  April first made them with her Grandma when she was a child.  Every year after that, she and her mom would make them around Christmas time.  She remembers being the one to flatten the cookies and her favorite part was dipping them in the chocolate.  She was always her mom's helper in the kitchen and she will always love those memories!*

## Chocolate Fudge Pie

½    (15 oz.) package refrigerated piecrusts
6      oz. unsweetened chocolate baking squares, chopped
1      (14 oz) can fat-free sweetened condensed milk
1    (8 oz.) container fat-free frozen whipped topping, thawed and divided
Garnish: fresh raspberries

Preheat oven to 425 degrees.  Fit pie crust into a 9-inch pie plate according to package directions.  Fold edges under, and crimp. Line pie crust with aluminum foil, and fill with pie weights or dried beans.  Bake at 425 degrees for 8 minutes.  Remove weights and foil, and bake 5 to 7 more minutes or until golden brown.  Cool good on a wire rack.   Meanwhile microwave chocolate in a large microwave-safe bowl on HIGH 1 minutes or until melted and smooth, stirring at 30-second intervals.  Whisk in milk until smooth.  Let stand 2 minutes.  Fold half of whipped topping into chocolate mixture until combined.  Pour mixture into crust.  Cover and chill 4 to 8 hours. Spread remaining whipped topping over pie.  Garnish, if desired.

*This dessert has been enjoyed by Damaris's family for many years. Her mother made it often.  Of course, when mother makes it, the recipe is always the best.*

## Chocolate Pecan Pie

3    eggs
¾    cup sugar
5    tbsp. melted butter (not margarine)
2    tsp. vanilla extract
¾    cup all purpose flour
1    cup of chocolate chip morsels
2   cups whole pecans pecan halves, not chopped (walnuts may be substituted)
1    unbaked Deep Dish pie shell, chilled but not frozen

Preheat oven to 350 degrees.  Beat eggs well.  Beat in sugar, butter, and vanilla.  Beat in flour.  Stir in chocolate chips and pecans. Bake at 350 for 40-45 minutes.   Cool for at least 2-3 hours...ENJOY!


*April's mother was a great cook, but never made pies.  However, her husband's family has deep southern roots, so pies were a common dessert, especially pecan pie.  His mother's best friend gave April this special recipe.  It's very easy and nearly impossible to mess up, so it was a great "first pie" for April to make.   It is a hit with everyone who has tried it!  It passed the taste test with the Titus ladies.*

## Chocolate Trifle

| | |
|---|---|
| 1 | box devil's food cake mix |
| 1 | large & 1 small Cool Whip |
| 1 | large pkg. dark chocolate instant pudding |
| 3 ½ | cups milk |
| 3 | Heath candy bars |

Bake cake as directed in a square pan. Cut small as for brownies. Mix pudding with the milk. Put candy bars in refrigerator. Cool, then crack into bits. Place a layer of cake in bottom of bowl. Cover with pudding, cool whip, and candy. Alternate layers of cake, pudding, Cool whip, and crumbled candy.

*This recipe given to Maggie by a very dear friend, Elaine Watson. Everyone needs a recipe like this one. It can be whipped up quickly and always turns out soooo good.*

## Collector's Cocoa Cake

| | |
|---|---|
| ¾ | cup butter |
| 1 ¾ | cup sugar |
| 2 | eggs |
| 1 | tsp. vanilla |
| 2 | cups all-purpose flour |
| ¾ | cup cocoa |
| 1 ¼ | tsp. baking powder |
| ½ | tsp. salt |
| 1 1/3 | cup water |

> *DeAnn makes great desserts, as this chocolate cake will prove  She says it is well worth the effort of preparation and could easily become one of your favorite cakes.*

Preheat oven to 350 degrees.  Grease and flour two 9  inch round baking pans.  Cream butter and sugar in large mixing bowl. Add eggs and vanilla and beat 1 min. at med. speed.   Combine flour, cocoa, baking powder and salt.  Add alternatively with water to creamed mixture, beating after each addition.  Pour batter into prepared pan.  Bake 30 to 35 minutes or until toothpick inserted in center comes out clean.  Cool 10 minutes.  Remove from pans and then cool completely.

Peanut Butter Frosting
| | |
|---|---|
| 8 | oz  cream  cheese |
| ½ | cup peanut butter |
| ¼ | cup butter, softened |
| 1 | lb. box powdered sugar |
| 1 | tsp.  vanilla |

In large mixing bowl beat cream cheese, peanut butter and butter until creamy.  Gradually add powdered sugar and vanilla, beating until blended.  Frost cake, cover and refrigerate.

## Cranberry-Nut Bread

| | |
|---|---|
| 2 | cups flour |
| ½ | tsp. salt |
| ½ | tsp. baking soda |
| 1½ | tsp. baking powder |
| 1 | cup sugar |
| ¾ | cups orange juice |
| 2 | tbsp. melted butter |
| 1 | beaten egg |
| 1 | cup cut up cranberries (fresh cranberries cut in half) |
| 1 | cup chopped nuts |

Sift together first 5 ingredients.  Mix together next 2 ingredients and add to first mixture. Mix last three ingredients and add to the mixture.   Bake at 325 degrees for 1 hour or until knife comes out clean.  Pour into a greased and floured loaf pan.  Sprinkle with cinnamon and sugar.

*This recipe of Nancy's mother was always a Christmas favorite with the family.  Nancy bakes a lot of small loaves of this bread at Christmas and shares it with so many others.  This is one of the ways she and Bob reach across the room  to show love for their neighbors.*

## Cream Cheese Pound Cake

3    sticks butter
3    cups powdered sugar, sifted
6    eggs
1    tsp. almond flavoring
1    package (8oz.) cream cheese, softened
1    tsp. vanilla
3    cups plain flour, sifted

     Cream together butter and cream cheese, blending in sugar. Add eggs, one at a time and keep on stirring. Add flavorings and flour. Beat until smooth, but do not overbeat. Pour batter into greased and floured tube pan. Bake at 325 degrees for 1 hour and 15 minutes, or until cake tests done.

*This is another old Southern favorite passed on to Maggie by her mother. Maggie's father was a minister and the family was always invited to someone's house for Sunday dinner and always had chicken and pound cake. Her mother always asked the hostess for the recipe to make her feel good. This one was a favorite and got passed on. The family still asks for "grandma" pound cake.*

*Some ole-timers say never to look at a pound cake until it has been in the oven for one hour.*

## Curried Blue Cheesecake

| | |
|---|---|
| 1 ¼ | cup butter-flavored cracker crumbs |
| ¼ | cup freshly grated parmesan cheese |
| ¼ | cup butter or margarine, melted |
| 3 | pkgs (8 oz.) softened cream cheese |
| 4 | eggs |
| ½ | cup mayonnaise |
| ½ | cup finely minced onion (substitute 3 large cloves of garlic) |
| 1 | tbsp. lemon juice |
| ¼ | tsp. curry powder |
| ½ | tsp. Worcestershire sauce |
| 8 | oz. crumbled blue cheese |

Major Grey's Mango Chutney (12-15 ounces)

Preheat oven to 300 degrees. Combine cracker crumbs, Parmesan cheese, and melted butter. Press into bottom of greased 9-inch spring form pan. Beat cream cheese until fluffy. Add eggs, one at a time, and beat 2 minutes after each addition. Continue beating while adding mayonnaise, onion, lemon juice, curry powder, and Worcestershire. Beat until well blended. Stir in blue cheese. Pour filling over crust. Bake 1-1/2 hours. Turn oven off. With oven door partially open, leave cheesecake in oven for 1 hour. Cool. Spoon Chutney over top of cheesecake. Serve chilled or at room temp with crackers.

*Karen says this is a two thumbs up! This delicious result will surely satisfy any cheesecake cravings and sooo easy to make. The recipe is a cinch to follow. You can replace some of the sugar with Splenda for lower calories.*

## Dear Abby's Pecan Pie

1    cup white corn syrup
1    cup dark brown sugar
1/3  cup melted butter
1    cup pecans
3    whole eggs
 Dash vanilla
 Pinch salt

      Mix above ingredients well.  Pour into pie shell and bake at 350 degrees for 45 to 50 minutes.  Cool and top with whipped cream or ice cream.  It is good served plain without the extra  calories.

*Maggie's mother loved to read "Dear Abby".  She cut out several of her articles.  (Maggie found them in her keepsakes).  She had gotten this outstanding recipe from one of those articles and it was made rather often.  When her mother was complimented on her delicious pecan pie, she always gave " Abby" the credit.  It is a good, good pie.*

## Easy Pecan Pie

1    cup dark syrup
¾  cup evaporated milk
1    cup chopped nuts
1    large package instant pudding
1    egg well beaten

     Combine syrup and pudding mix in bowl. Add milk and egg, stirring to blend. Add pecans. Pour into pie shell. Bake at 375 degrees for 55 minutes.

*Shannon's pecan pie passed the taste test with flying colors. Other than banana pudding, pecan pie has been a southern favorite since the "Sherman" days, and more and more recipes keep popping up. Try them all, especially with a good dab of whipped cream.*

## Fig Cookies

1    cup butter, softened
2    cups brown sugar
2    eggs
1    tbsp. vanilla
4    cups all purpose flour
1    tsp. baking soda dissolved in ½ cup of water
1    cup fig preserves/can use fresh mashed figs
Pinch of salt

In a large mixing bowl, combine all ingredients except figs. Roll 2/3 of the batter into small balls and place on a cookie sheet. Returns about 35 cookies.  Imprint thumb in each cookie ball and fill with figs.  Top each cookie with remaining batter.  Cook at 350 degrees for 10 to 13 minutes.  Turn  over and cook again for 10 to 13 minutes for a more crispy cookie.  These tend to get soft and moist so may need to crisp up in the oven again a few days later.  After first cooking, you can cook two more times.

Nancy finds *these tasty cookies are better after a few days.  There are not many recipes using figs, but this one is a winner.*

## Fresh Apple Cake

3     large or 4 cups diced apples (with skin)
2     cups sugar
1     cup chopped nuts.
       Mix together and set aside for 1 hour.
3     cups flour
1     tsp. salt
2     tsp. baking soda
1     tsp. cinnamon
       Sift together and add to first mixture
1     cup cooking oil
2     eggs
1     tsp. vanilla extract

Bake in a tube pan (greased and floured) for 1 hour and 15 minutes at 325 degrees. Insert knife to see if done. Let cool in pan before removing. Also can bake in 2 loaf pans.

*Nancy rates this as a light, not too sweet dessert, but very, very good. It has received great raves when served.*

*Never use anything to grease a cake pan or dish but shortening.*

## Fresh Blueberry Pie

¾     cup sugar
2 ½  tbsp. corn starch
½     tsp. salt
2/3  cup water
3     cups fresh blueberries (1 pint)
2     tbsp. butter
1 ½  tbsp. lemon juice
1     (8oz) cool whip (lite)
1     Pastry shell (bake)

      Combine sugar, cornstarch and salt.  Blend in water and 1 cup blueberries.  Bring to boil.  Cook stirring constantly until very thick.  Stir in butter and lemon juice.  Cool.  Fold in remaining blueberries and chill 1 hour.  Spread half cool whip on bottom of pie shell.  Pour in filling.  Spread on other half of cool whip.  Chill 1-2 hours before serving.

*All the cooks gave this recipe two thumbs up!*

*Studies of Blueberries have found that they trigger neu-rons (nerve connectors) that keep the brain sharp.  "Old neurons are like old married couples.  They don't talk to one another very well anymore."  Suddenly, the humble Blueberry shows up, and brightens things up in the brain. Eat more blueberries!*

## Hot Fudge Pudding Cake

| | |
|---|---|
| ¾ | cup sugar |
| 1 | cup all-purpose flour |
| ¼ | cup cocoa powder |
| 2 | tsp. baking powder |
| ¼ | tsp. salt |
| ½ | cup milk |
| 1/3 | cup butter, melted |
| 1 ½ | tsp. vanilla |
| ½ | cup sugar |
| ½ | cup light brown sugar, packed |
| ¼ | cup cocoa powder |
| 1 ¼ | cup hot water |

Preheat oven to 350°. Combine the first 5 ingredients; stir in milk, butter and vanilla; beat until smooth. Pour batter into ungreased 9 inch square pan. Stir together remaining 3 ingredients; sprinkle mixture evenly over batter. Pour hot water over top; do not stir. Bake 35 to 40 minutes or until center is almost set. Remove from oven; let stand 15 minutes before serving. Best served warm; serve with whipped topping or ice cream.

*Damaris says this is her husband's favorite dessert. It has been his birthday cake of choice since he was very young. This cake makes it own sauce as it cooks.*

## Humming Bird Cake With Cream Cheese Frosting

1 1/2   cups canola oil
3       cups flour
2       cups sugar
1       tsp. salt
1       tsp. baking soda
1       tsp. cinnamon
1 ½    tsp. vanilla extract
1       (8oz.) can crushed pineapple (undrained)
3       eggs beaten
1       cup chopped nuts
2       cups mashed bananas

Combine dry ingredients, then add beaten eggs and oil (do not beat too much). Add remaining ingredients and stir in. Bake in two round greased and floured cake pans at 350 degrees for 30 minutes. Spread on cream cheese frosting.

Cream Cheese Frosting
2       (8oz.) pkg. cream cheese, softened
2       (16 oz.) pkg. confectioners' sugar
2       tbsp. vanilla extract

Mix all ingredients until smooth and fluffy. Add milk if necessary for spreading consistency.

*Nancy has shared this cake with our group many times at our monthly get-togethers. We all devour it. It really is a delicious cake and looks so pretty. It has won the blue ribbon at many country fairs.*

## Johnny Cake

Cake batter:
| | |
|---|---|
| 1/2 | cup butter |
| 2 | cups sugar |
| 1 | egg |

    Beat until fluffy

| | |
|---|---|
| 2 1/2 | cups flour |
| 2 | tsp baking powder |
| 1 | cup milk |

> ### No Fail Pie Crust
> 4 cups flour
> 1 3/4 cups shortening
> 1 egg
> 1 tbsp vinegar
> 1 tbsp sugar
> 1/2 cup water
> Mix and roll.  Makes 3 large pies.

    Alternating dry & wet ingredients, mix till smooth.  Pour into pie crusts. Preheat oven now to 425 degrees.

Juice:
| | |
|---|---|
| 1 | cup molasses (King or Turkey) |
| 1 | tsp flour |
| 1 | egg |
| 1 | tsp vanilla |

    Mix/beat together all ingredients, then....(pay attention now), take

1   cup BOILING water and carefully add 1 tsp baking soda. Mix immediately with juice mixture. Place pies with batter on rack in oven.  Carefully pour juice on top of batter in pie crusts. Slowly push rack into oven and bake at 425 for 10 minutes.  Reduce oven to 375 degrees until done, 30—45 minutes.  Use toothpick to test- a little moist ok, top will be browned.  Do not over cook.  Kelly likes to make a little more juice (or goo) and use deep dish pie pans.  May need to reduce some of the cake batter to make room for extra goo.  Kelly recommends homemade crust, make sure there are no holes!

*This recipe from Kelly's grandmother is one of her family's favorites. She has searched online, but cannot find another like it under this same name.  There are other Johnny cakes, but they're more like a pancake. It may take a few tries to get the chemistry right, but you won't mind trying!*

## Lemon Crunch Pound Cake

1 ¾  cups sugar
2      cups cake flour
1       cup oil
2      tsp. lemon flavoring
5      large eggs

Cream sugar and oil thoroughly.  Add eggs (one at a time).  Add flavoring .  Add cake flour that has been sifted 4 times.  Bake in tube pan 1 hour at 350 degrees.

*Everyone needs this recipe in their file.  The cake has a crunchy top and is oh so good.  It is easy to put together for last minute company. Husbands love this cake.  Bake it and make his day.*

*Always preheat oven for at least 10 minutes unless otherwise stated in recipe.*

## Lemon Delight

Bottom Layer:
1½   cup flour
½    cup chopped nuts
1½   sticks of butter

Crumble and press in 9 x 13 pan.  Bake at 375 degrees for 15 minutes.

Second Layer:
1      cup confectionary sugar
1      (8oz.) package softened cream cheese.
1      cup whipped cream
    Blend together and spread on first cooled layer
Third Layer:
2      pkg. instant lemon pudding
3      cups milk.
    Blend and spread on second  layer and chill
Top Layer:
1    cup whipped cream and spread on top.  Chill and keep refrigerated.

    *Nancy shares another of her mom's  recipes that has been in her family for a long time.  What is so nice about the old recipes is that they are passed down in the family, and never get worn out. This is an excellent refreshing dessert to make for the family game nights.  Make enough for seconds.*

## Lemon Meringue Pie

| | |
|---|---|
| 1 | baked 8 or 9 inch pie shell |
| 1 | cup granulated sugar |
| ¼ | cup cornstarch |
| 1/8 | tsp. salt |
| 1 ¼ | cups warm water |
| 1 | grated lemon rind |
| ¼ | cup lemon juice |
| 3 | egg yolks, slightly beaten |
| 1 | tbsp. butter or margarine |

In double boiler combine sugar, cornstarch, and salt. Slowly stir in water, then lemon rind and juice, egg yolks, and butter. Cook, stirring until smooth and thick enough to mound when dropped from spoon. Remove from heat. Cool thoroughly. Start heating oven to 350 degrees. Spoon filling into cooled pie shell. Top with meringue. Bake to 12 to 15 minutes.

*Testing proved this to be a very good lemon pie. Audrey says it is an old recipe that has been passed down from generation to generation. Some recipes just stay good and never lose their taste.*

## Lemon Squares

½     cup margarine, melted
1      cup flour
2      eggs
1 ½  cups brown sugar, packed
2      tbsp.  lemon juice
1      tsp. grated lemon rind
½     tsp. salt
1      cup flaked coconut
½     cup pecans, chopped

Mix margarine, ½ cup brown sugar (packed), flour and press into 9 x 13 pan.  Bake at 350 degrees for 20-25 minutes or until lightly browned.  Cool.  Ice with 1 cup powdered sugar, 1 tbsp. lemon juice and 2 tbsp. margarine (melted).

*Karen  was given this recipe from a dear friend.  Lemon squares are always tasty and a good dessert  to take to a covered dish get-together.*

## Maggie's Easy Divinity Candy

1     pkg.  Betty Crocker vanilla frosting mix
2/3   cup karo syrup
1     tsp. vanilla
1     pkg. (16) oz powdered sugar
1 ½   cups chopped pecans

    Blend frosting mix, syrup and  vanilla  in large mixing bowl. With mixer at low speed or by hand, gradually blend in sugar.  It may take a little water (not over ¼ cup) to keep mixing.   If mixing with mixer gets too hard, finish the job by hand beating.

When mixed thoroughly stir in nuts.  Drop mixture by teaspoon on lightly buttered wax paper.   Allow to dry for 12 hours, then turn over and let bottom dry for another 12 hours.   Very good but must warn you, it is not low in calories.

*This is a very easy way to prepare this delicious candy and it receives raves when served.  Maggie treats all the family to a can of this candy every Christmas.*

## Mandy's Candy Bar Pie

1    9 inch pie crust, unbaked
5    bars snickers (2.07 oz. each)
¼    cup sugar
4    pkgs. (3 oz. each) cream cheese softened—12 oz. total
2    eggs
1/3  cup sour cream
1/3  cup creamy peanut butter
3    tbsp. heavy cream
2/3  cup chocolate chips

   Preheat oven to 450 degrees.  Using a 9 inch pie pan, bake pie crust 5-7 minutes or until very light golden brown.  Remove from oven and let cool.  Reduce oven temperature to 325 degrees.  Meanwhile, cut candy bars in half lengthwise, then cut into ¼ inch pieces. Place candy bar pieces over bottom of partially baked crust.  In a small bowl, combine the sugar and cream cheese.  Beat until smooth. Add eggs 1 at a time, beating well after each addition.  Add sour cream and peanut butter, beating until mixture is smooth.  Pour over candy bar pieces.  Bake 30-40 minutes, or until  center is set.  Cool completely.  When pie is cooled, heat the heavy cream in a small saucepan until very warm.  Remove from heat and stir in chocolate chips.  Stir until chips are melted and mixture is smooth.  Spread over top of cooled pie.  Refrigerate 2-3 hours before serving.  Store in refrigerator.

*Mandy, Pastor Jay Thompson's wife, wanted to share this recipe with everyone.  It's one of her favorites.*

## Mocha Brownies with Coffee Frosting

Brownies
6        squares unsweetened chocolate (1 oz squares)
2        tbsp. instant coffee granules
1½      cup butter
2 ¼     cup  sugar
5        eggs, large
2        cups  all-purpose flour
1        tsp. vanilla  extract
½       tsp. salt

*DeAnn wants all of you to try this old favorite passed down through her family. It is a  hit with the young folks as well as with the old.  These brownies are everything a brownie should be.  Good, good and good.*

   Preheat oven to 350°.  Line a 13x9x2 inch baking pan with alumi-num foil.  In a medium bowl, combine butter and chocolate.  Microwave on high in 30 second intervals, stirring between each, until chocolate is melted and smooth.  Stir coffee granules into melted chocolate until dissolved.  In a large bowl, combine chocolate mixture and sugar.  Beat at medium speed until well blended.  Add eggs, one at a time, beating well after each addi-tion.  Add flour, vanilla, and salt, beating until just combined.  Spread bat-ter into prepared pan.  Bake 40 minutes, or until a wooden pick inserted in center comes out still slightly sticky.  Cool completely in pan on wire rack; remove from foil.  Spread frosting on top of brownies.

Coffee Frosting
 ½      cup semisweet chocolate morsels
4        oz. cream cheese, softened
2        tbsp. butter, softened
2        tbsp. strong brewed espresso or coffee
1         tsp. vanilla extract
2½     cups confectioners' sugar
   In a small bowl, microwave chocolate morsels on high in 30 second intervals, stirring between each, until chocolate is melted and smooth.  Cool chocolate slightly.  In a medium bowl, combine cream cheese and but-ter.  Beat at medium speed with until creamy.  Add chocolate, espresso or coffee and vanilla, beating until well blended.  Gradually beat in confection-ers' sugar until smooth.

## Nutty Orange Coffee Cake

¾    cup granulated sugar
½    cup chopped pecans
2    tsp. grated orange rind
1    (8oz.) pkg. cream cheese
2    (11 oz.) cans refrigerated buttermilk biscuits
½    cup butter, melted
1    cup sifted powdered sugar
2    tbsp. fresh orange juice

Combine first 3 ingredients in small bowl and set aside. Place about 1 tsp. cream cheese on half of each biscuit. Fold biscuit over cheese, pressing edges to seal. Dip biscuits in melted butter and dredge in the sugar mixture (the first 3 ingredients). Place curved side down in a greased 12-cup Bundt pan, spacing evenly. Drizzle any remaining butter over biscuits. Sprinkle with remaining sugar mixture. Bake 350 degrees for 40 minutes or until done. Immediately invert onto a plate. Combine powdered sugar and orange juice. Drizzle over warm cake. Makes one 10-inch cake

*Tam says this is an easy way to cook a good coffee cake. It may be a little messy to eat but it is so good.*

## Oatmeal Cookies

| | |
|---|---|
| 2 | cups butter |
| 24 | oz. chocolate chips |
| 4 | cups flour |
| 2 | cups brown sugar |
| 2 | tsp. soda |
| 1 | tsp. salt |
| 2 | cups sugar |
| 8 | oz. Grated Cadbury chocolate |
| 5 | cups blended oatmeal |
| 4 | eggs |
| 2 | tsp. baking powder |
| 2 | tsp. vanilla |
| 3 | cups chopped nuts (optional) |

Measure oatmeal, and blend in a blender to a fine powder. Cream the butter and both sugars. Add eggs and vanilla, mix together with flour, oatmeal, salt, baking powder, and bicarbonate of soda. Add chocolate chips, grated chocolate and nuts. Roll into balls and place two inches apart on a cookie sheet. Bake for 10 minutes at 375 degrees (180 C). Yield: about 112 cookies.

*This is a famous recipe from Neiman Marcus. It was sent by email from someone who paid $250.00 for the recipe. We thought you may want to bake these to see if they are really worth the money, or if you would be paying for the name "Neiman Marcus".*

## Old Fashion Biscuit Pudding

| | |
|---|---|
| 10 | canned or homemade biscuits |
| ¾ | cup sugar |
| ½ | cup raisins |
| ¼ | tsp. cloves |
| 3 | eggs |
| 1 ½ | cups milk |
| 1 | tsp. vanilla |

Slice biscuits and slightly butter each side.  Arrange in 6 x 9 inch baking dish.  Sprinkle each layer with cinnamon cloves and raisins.  Beat eggs with sugar.  Add  milk and vanilla.  Pour mixture over biscuits.  If more liquid is needed to come through layers of biscuits, pour milk around edges of dish.  Do not cover top layer. Bake at 350 degrees until custard is set and top is slightly browned.

### Optional Topping

| | |
|---|---|
| 1 | cup  mincemeat |
| 1 | tsp.  butter |
| 3 | tsp.  brown sugar |
| ¼ | cup  water |

Mix all ingredients in small sauce pan and simmer until bubbly. Spoon over individual serving of hot pudding.

*There are always several pudding recipes in a cookbook  This one is a nice change from the usual and very easy to prepare.  It is especially enjoyable for the mincemeat lovers.*

## Old Fashion Ginger Snaps

| | |
|---|---|
| 2 | cups sorghum molasses |
| 1 | cup melted butter |
| ½ | cup brown sugar |
| 1 | cup hot water |
| 1 | cup flour |
| ½ | tsp. red pepper |
| 2 | tsp. soda |
| 2 | tsp. ginger |

Mix molasses, butter, sugar and hot water. Mix together the remaining ingredients and add to the molasses mixture. If necessary, add more flour. Roll out thin on floured cloth. Cut with a small round cookie cutter. Place on greased cookie sheet. Bake at 35 degrees until brown. Store in tight tin container.

*This is a good recipe for Ginger Snaps, which are not homemade very often. Most of us still remember when our mothers made them from scratch rather than buying them from the store.*

## Panettone Bread Pudding

4    large eggs
1    qt. canned or refrigerated eggnog
8    cups cubed panettones (1 pound Italian cookie tarts)

      Heat oven to 350 degrees.  Coat a 2-qt. shallow baking dish with nonstick spray.  Whisk eggs in a large bowl until blended.  Whisk in the eggnog.  Place panettone cubes in prepared baking dish.  Pour the eggnog mixture over the top to coat.  Bake, uncovered for 50 to 55 minutes until knife inserted in center comes out clean.  Serve warm or at room temperature.  Sprinkle with confectioners' sugar if desired.  Serves 8.

*Hopefully you will be able to find the Panettones.  This is a very delicious dessert that everyone will enjoy.*

## Pastor Lee's Perfect Pound Cake

3   cups regular flour – (Swans Down)
3   cups sugar
2   sticks of **real** butter (soften to room temp)
8   oz. of sour cream (sometimes I will add an extra teaspoon or so.)
6   eggs (room temp)
¼   tsp. baking soda
1   tsp. vanilla (recipe calls for ¼ tsp., but I use about 1 tsp.)

Preheat oven to 325 degrees.  Grease and flour cake pan.  Sift flour.  Mix sugar and butter.  Add ingredients. (I usually add a little bit of each ingredient until all are used.  Then I mix for another 2 minutes or so.)  Pour into cake pan (be sure and leave enough for you to enjoy the batter! It should taste really good – if not you messed up!)  Cook for approximately 1 hour 20 minutes.  (This will depend on your oven)

*The Senior Pastor at Lakeside, Lee Ross, thinks he might be able to cook this pound cake almost as good as his mother-in-law.*

## Peanut Butter Blossoms

48      Hershey Kisses
½       cup shortening
¾       cup Reese's creamy peanut butter
1/2   cup granulated sugar
1/2   cup packed light brown sugar
1       egg
2       tbsp.  milk
1       tsp. vanilla extract
1 ½   cups all-purpose flour
1       tsp.  baking soda
½       tsp. salt
½       cup granulated sugar
½       cup brown sugar

Preheat oven to 375 degrees and remove wrappers from chocolates.  Beat shortening and peanut butter in large bowl until well blended.  Add ½ cup granulated sugar and brown sugar.  Beat until fluffy.  Add egg, milk and vanilla.  Beat well.  Stir together flour, baking soda and salt.  Gradually beat into peanut mixture.  Shape dough into 1-inch balls.  Roll in granulated sugar.  Place on ungreased cookie sheet.  Bake 8 to 10 minutes or until lightly browned.  Immediately press a chocolate into center of each cookie.  Cookie will crack around edges.  Remove from cookie sheet to wire rack.  Cool completely.  Makes about 4 dozen cookies.

*Amy shares with us a delicious cookie recipe.  These are a must try, and both children and adults will enjoy.  Nothing can take the place of homemade cookies.*

# Fed by Grace

## Peanut Butter Cookies

1     yellow cake mix
1     cup peanut butter
1/2  cup cooking oil
2     tbsp. water
2     eggs

Preheat oven to 350 degrees.  Combine all ingredients, mix well. Drop from spoon onto an ungreased cookie sheet.  Make a cross on each using a fork. Make sure to dip in water in between each cookie.  Bake for 10-12 minutes or until golden.  Cool on cookie sheet for about 1 minute then remove them. Place on cooling rack.  Can add nuts or replace peanut butter with chocolate chips. You can change it up!

*Damaris shares this family recipe that her mom, Debbie Hester, has used for years.  Damaris's daughter, Kourtni, used it in a fairytale cookbook in the 1st grade. She made them with chocolate chips and called them "Cinderella's Chocolate Chip Cookies".*

> *When you get to your wit's end, you'll find God lives there.*

## Peanut Butter Fingers

### Crust

| | |
|---|---|
| ½ | cup sugar |
| ½ | cup brown sugar, packed |
| 1 | cup all-purpose flour |
| 1 | cup quick cooking oats, uncooked |
| 1/3 | cup peanut butter |
| 1 | egg |
| ½ | tsp. vanilla |
| ½ | cup butter, melted |

### Icing

| | |
|---|---|
| ½ | cup  peanut Butter |
| 2 | tbsp.  cocoa |
| ½ | box powdered sugar |
| As needed | milk |

Combine sugar, flour and oatmeal in bowl.  Cut in peanut butter.  Add egg, vanilla and butter; mix well.  Press into a well greased 9 x 11 in pan.  Bake at 350° for 15 to 20 minutes.  For icing, combine peanut butter, sugar and cocoa; add milk gradually until creamy.  Spread icing over crust.  Makes 20.

*This  recipe comes from Francis Hester, DeAnn's Great Grand-mother.  These cookies have always been a favorite of DeAnn and she's been eating them since early childhood.*

## Pirate's House Carolina Trifle

1   (6 ounce) box vanilla pudding (instant or regular)
3   cups milk
1   cup sherry
½ pint heavy cream
2   tbsp. granulated sugar
¼ tsp. vanilla extract
Angel food cake

Mix pudding and milk according to package directions and refrigerate until thickened. Add sherry and blend well. Then refrigerate. Whip the cream with sugar and vanilla until it stands in soft peaks (not too stiff). With serrated knife slice cake horizontally in ½ inch thick slices. Pour half the pudding into a glass soufflé dish or serving dish. Cover with a layer of cake slices, piercing them together to fit. Cover cake with half the whipped cream. Repeat with pudding, cake and whipped cream. Cover and refrigerate.

*This recipe was given to Maggie by Herb Traub in the early 1950's. He was owner of The Pirate's House, a very old and famous restaurant in Savannah, Ga. The city is known for its outstanding restaurants and you should visit one of these, such as the Pirate's House, Lady and Sons (Paula Deen), Mrs. Wilkes Boarding House, 1790 Restaurant, Johnny Harris, and Elizabeth on 37th. These have received great acclaim from visitors all over the world.*

## Pound Cake, 1-2-3-4

1       cup butter
2       cups sugar
3       cups sifted cake flour
1       cup milk
4       eggs
2       tsp. baking powder
1 ½    tbsp. lemon extract

Cream the butter and sugar and add eggs.  Mix well.
Alternately add the milk and flour and baking powder that has been
sifted together.  Add lemon extract.  Pour into greased and floured
tube pan and bake at 350 degrees for one hour.

Orange Cream Cheese Frosting
    6    oz. cream cheese
    ½    cup orange juice concentrate
    6    tbsp. butter
    4    cups sifted confectioners' sugar
    Dash salt

Cream butter and cheese until light and fluffy.  Add orange juice, salt,
and confectioners' sugar until of spreading consistency.  Blend
thoroughly.

*When Barbara entered the Ohio Mrs. America pageant ( homemaking contest) in her early marriage, she was required to prepare two dishes for the judges.  This pound cake was the one that she chose to cook and must have been an outstanding presentation because she was one of the winners in the contest.*

## Pumpkin Honey Bread

1    cup pure honey
½  cup butter softened
1    can (16 oz.) solid pack pumpkin
4    eggs
4    cups flour
4    tsp. baking powder
2    tsp. ground cinnamon
2    tsp.  ground ginger
1    tsp. t baking soda
1    tsp. salt
1    tsp. ground nutmeg

In a large bowl, cream honey with butter until light and fluffy. Stir in pumpkin.  Beat in eggs, one at a time, until thoroughly blended.  Sift together remaining ingredients.  Stir into pumpkin mixture.  Divide batter equally between two well greased loaf pans. Bake at 350 degrees for 1 hour or until a tooth pick inserted in the center comes out clean.  Let loaves cook in pan for 10 minutes before taking out of pans to cool on racks.

*Nancy makes her favorite breads and shares them with others on holidays and at Christmas.  This is one of her favorites.*

## Sara's Cocoa Brownies

½   cup sugar
½   cup brown sugar
½   cup butter or margarine
1    tsp. vanilla
2    eggs
2/3  cup self-rising flour
½   cup cocoa
½   cup chopped walnuts (optional)

Mix sugar, butter, vanilla and eggs. Stir in remaining ingredients. Spread in greased 8x8 pan. Cook at 350 degrees, 25-30 minutes.

*Audrey shares her favorite brownie recipe. Her children love them, but what child does not enjoy a brownie.*

## Scotch Short Bread

¼   lb. sugar
½   lb. butter
1    lb. flour

      Cream butter and sugar and add warmed flour gradually. Knead thoroughly as for bread. Cut as desired. Work into cakes with hands on paper. Notch edges with fork and prick top with fork. Cook in cool oven about 250 to 300 degrees for 25 to 30 minutes. Watch until pale yellow (easy to burn).

*There is nothing better than a good shortbread. Karen wants you to try this easy cookie recipe. You can't eat just one. One calls for another and another.*

## Scripture Cake

3 ½    cups 1 Kings 4:22 (flour)
1       cup Judg. 5:25, last clause (butter)
2       cups Jer. 6:20 (sugar)
2       cups Nahum 3:12 (raisins)
2       cups Num. 17:8 (almonds)
½      cup Judg. 4:19, last clause (milk)
1       tbsp. 1 Sam. 14:25 (honey)
2       tsps. Amos 4:5, leavening  (baking powder)
6       of Jer. 10:11 (eggs)
1       tbsp.  each of spices (allspice, cinnamon, and nutmeg)
Season to taste with 2 Chronicles 9:19 (spices)

Cream together the butter and sugar until light and very fluffy. Add the sifted flour, baking powder, salt and spices alternately with the milk and honey.  Dredge the raisins and figs in a very small amount of flour, and then stir in, along with the almonds (chopped very fine).  Pour into a large greased and floured tube pan.  Bake at 300 degrees for around an hour and 30 minutes, or until it tests done.

*Maggie's mother made this recipe often.  She would take it to church and share with her Sunday School Class.  As they were eating it, she would ask different ones to read the scriptures that referenced  the cake.  She was sometimes called the "scripture cake lady".*

## Seven Minute Frosting

3    egg whites
¾   cup sugar
¾   cup white corn syrup
1    tbsp. water
½   tsp. vanilla

Combine all ingredients except vanilla.  Place over boiling water.  Cook 7 minutes beating constantly with the mixer.  Remove from the heat and stir in the vanilla.  Provides enough icing for a 9 inch cake.

*Outstanding icing recipe!  You can sometimes add coconut as well as chopped pecans.  It's good on any flavor of cake.*

## Skillet Peach or Blueberry Dumplings

¼    cup butter
¼    cup sugar
1    tbsp. sugar
1 ¼  cup flour
2    tsp. baking powder
¼    tsp. salt + 1 T. sugar
¼    cup shortening (or softened butter)
2/3  cup milk
5    fresh peaches, halved (or 2-3 cups of blueberries)

Melt butter in skillet. Sprinkle ¼ cup sugar over butter. Lay the peach halves cut side down and sprinkle with 1 tbsp. sugar. Sift flour 3 times with baking powder, salt and 1 tbsp. sugar. Cut in shortening. Add milk and beat well. Spoon batter over peaches. Bake at 375 degrees for 35 minutes or until golden brown. Serve hot with some vanilla ice cream on top.

*Nancy can come up with some mouth-watering recipes. This one is a good take off from cobblers. Serve this when you want to be a little different.*

## Southern Bread Pudding

1 ¼    cups low-fat (1%) milk
4      large eggs
1/3    cup sugar
2      tsp. vanilla extract
½      tsp. cinnamon
1/8    tsp. ground nutmeg
12     slices cinnamon-raisin bread, crusts discarded, bread cut into 1
-inch squares
3      tbsp. chopped pecans

    Preheat oven to 350 degrees.  Spray  1 ½ quart shallow baking dish with nonstick spray.  Combine the milk, eggs, sugar, vanilla extract, cinnamon, and nutmeg in a large bowl; whisk until blended.  Add the bread, apple, and pecans.  Let the mixture stand, stirring occasionally, until the bread absorbs some of the liquid, about 10 minutes.  Pour the mixture into the baking dish.  Bake until the pudding is puffed and a knife inserted into the center comes out clean, 25-30 minutes.  Remove the pudding from the oven and let cool 15 minutes.  Serve warm.


*This is another recipe from the "plantation cooks" in Albany, Ga. Bread pudding is always a favorite when company drops in.*

## Sweet Potato Cheesecake

> *DeAnn ate a cheese-cake similar to this at a local restaurant and decided to recreate it at home. She feels she has come close with this one.*

| | |
|---|---|
| 1 ¼ | cup graham cracker crumbs |
| ¼ | cup sugar |
| ¼ | cup butter, melted |
| ½ | tsp cinnamon |

Filling

| | |
|---|---|
| 2 | lbs sweet potatoes (need 2 cups puree) |
| ¼ | cup packed brown sugar |
| ½ | tsp. cinnamon |
| ¼ | tsp. nutmeg |
| ¼ | tsp. ginger |
| 2 | tsp. vanilla |
| 3 | pkgs. cream cheese, softened (8oz pkg) |
| 1 | tbsp. white sugar |
| ⅓ | cup sour cream |
| ¼ | cup heavy whipping cream |
| 3 | eggs |

Topping

| | |
|---|---|
| ¾ | cup packed brown sugar |
| ¼ | cup butter |
| ¼ | cup whipping cream |
| 1 | cup chopped pecans or walnuts |

Preheat oven to 350 degrees F. Mix together graham cracker crumbs, sugar, butter and cinnamon. Press mixture into the bottom of a 9½-inch spring form pan. Bake 10 minutes. Cool. Place potatoes in a baking dish. Bake until a knife inserted in center goes through in center goes through easily, about an hour. Cool potatoes, peel and puree. Transfer 2 cups of sweet potato puree to a large mixing bowl. Add brown sugar, cinnamon, nutmeg, ginger, vanilla, cream cheese, sugar, sour cream and whipping cream; beat until smooth. Beat in eggs one at a time. Pour filling into crust. Bake until tester inserted in center comes out clean, about an hour. Combine brown sugar and butter in a small saucepan. Stir until sugar dissolves. Increase heat, and bring to a boil. Mix in whipping cream, then nuts. Pour hot topping over cheesecake. Refrigerate.

## Sweet Potato Pie

| | |
|---|---|
| 6-8 | medium yams or 1 ½ cups canned yams |
| 1 | tsp. Vanilla |
| 1 ½ | cups undiluted evaporated milk |
| ½ | stick butter |
| 8 | tsp. brown sugar |
| ½ | tsp. ginger |
| ½ | cup corn syrup |
| 1 | tsp. cinnamon |
| ½ | tsp.  nutmeg |
| 3 | eggs separated |

9 in baked pastry shell with high rim

Mash yams adding vanilla, milk and butter.  Blend all other ingredients, except egg whites in large bowl.  Add potato mixture and whip until light.  Fold in beaten egg white.  Pour mixture into pie shell.  Bake in oven 45 minutes at 375 degrees.

*This is a very good sweet potato pie.  The recipe has been around for a very long time.*

## Pumpkin Pie First Grade Style

A   *tray*
A   *pumpkin*
     *some butter*

Buy a pumpkin. Put the pumpkin on the tray for five minutes on the stove. Turn the stove on. Let it bake for six minutes. We take it out. We let it cool. We eat it.

*We just wanted to share another Pumpkin Pie recipe from Lake Oconee Academy's First Grade student, Kassie.*

## Tropical Pineapple Cake

| | |
|---|---|
| 2 | cups sugar |
| 2 | cups all-purpose flour |
| ½ | cup vegetable oil |
| 2 | eggs |
| 1 | tsp.  baking soda |
| 1 | 20-ounce can crushed pineapple with juice |

In a medium bowl, combine all of the ingredients .  Pour into a well-greased 13 x 9-inch pan.  Bake at 350 degrees for 25 minutes or until a cake tester comes out clean.

To make this cake in layers, divide the batter between three 9-inch cake pans.  Bake in 350 degree preheated oven for approximately 22 minutes or until a cake tester comes out clean from the center of the cake.

Icing

| | |
|---|---|
| 1 | cup sugar |
| ½ | butter, softened |
| 2/3 | cup evaporated milk (1 small can) |
| | pinch of salt |
| ½ | cup pecans, chopped |
| ½ | cup coconut |

In a saucepan, combine the sugar, butter, milk, and salt. Bring to a boil and then lower the heat.  Cook and stir for 10 minutes. Remove the pan from the heat.  Add the pecans and coconut.  For the sheet cake, pour the icing over the hot cake and allow it to cool before cutting.  For the layer cake, allow layers to cool slightly; Spread about ½ cup icing between layers, and place the remaining icing on top.  If you really want to make it a hit, put seven-minute icing all over the cake.

Finally.....here is an easy, delicious cake for those pineapple lovers. It is lower in fat than other cakes. It makes a great show and is just the right cake to take to a church "dinner on the ground", a family reunion, or dinner parties.

# Smoothies
## & other Misc Foods

Smoothies are known to maintain and repair many parts of our bodies. Fruits and vegetables in our diet can be one of the best defenses against stress, disease and infections. They provide our bodies with the necessary nutrients and vitamins that aid in the digestion of food, nerve and muscle functions, healing and fighting infections and maintaining regular heart beat. For a relaxing treat, mix up and drink some good tasting smoothies with lots of fruits and vegetables to help our bodies stay young and feeling great.

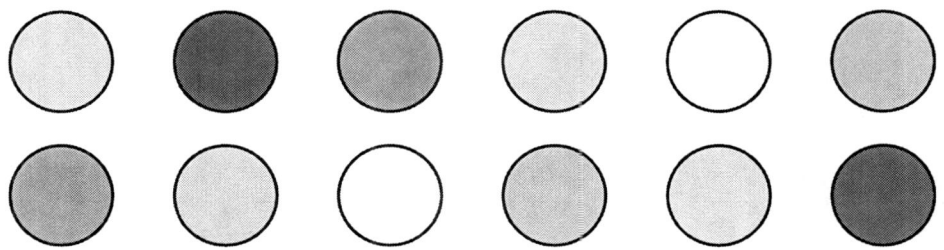

## Banana Break Smoothie

1    sliced banana
1    cup limeade
1    cup lime sherbet
½   cup non-fat banana yogurt
2    cups ice

*This creamy smoothie is very tasty and provides all the potassium that your body needs during stressful times.*

## Carbo Creation Smoothie

1       cup apple juice
1       cup slice peaches
¼      cup blueberries
½      cup strawberries
1       cup vanilla yogurt
2 ½   cups ice

*This smoothie is filled with carbohydrates to achieve your energy needs during strenuous exercise.*

## Coffee Punch

3    cups boiling water
½    cup sugar
4    tbsp. instant coffee (regular or decaf), not International Foods
     though
6    tbsp. Hershey's chocolate syrup
¼    tsp. salt

Mix all this together and let cool in fridge for at least 2 hours, preferably overnight.  About 30 minutes before you are ready to serve the punch, pour the above cooled liquid into a punch bowl and add: 1 quart milk, 12 oz. ginger ale, 11/2 gallon vanilla ice cream (cut into large cubes).  This will fill a small punch bowl.

*This was furnished by Karen.  Anyone looking for an unusual punch will find this to be just what you are looking for.*

## **Egg Nog**

6    eggs (separated)
¼    cup granulated sugar (for whites)
½    cup granulated sugar (for yellows)
1    Qt. of half and half
Optional (Brandy, Rum and Nutmeg)

Separate eggs. Make sure no yellow is in egg whites. Beat egg whites until stiff peaks form. Add ¼ cup of sugar after whites are stiff and beat until shiny stiff. Beat yolks until creamy yellow with ½ cup sugar. Beat until well aerated. Put whites in very cold punch bowl trying not to lose air. Fold in egg yolk mixture gently trying not to deflate whites. Serve very cold with brandy, whiskey and/or rum and nutmeg (fresh ground if possible) as desired. Be sure not to contaminate the whites with yolk or they will not beat properly.

*Best egg nog ever! and is very easy to prepare.*

## Sour Cream Sauce

Beat 1/3 cup butter, softened, and 1 cup powdered sugar at medium speed with an electric mixer until smooth.  Add ½ cup sour cream, ½ tsp. lemon juice, and ¼ tsp. vanilla, beating until creamy.  Cover and chill until ready to serve (up to 8 hours).  Makes about 1 ¾ cups.

*This is a delicious sauce to have on hand.  It can add an appetizing taste to many dishes.  This would be superb on a baked potato, topped with herbs, and fruit dishes.*

## Trey's Hollandaise Sauce

2     sticks of unsalted butter
6     egg yolks
1 ½ tbsp. lemon juice
1     tsp. salt

Cut butter in smaller pieces and melt in a double boiler over medium-low heat.   Do not allow water in double boiler to come to a boil.  Butter will be too hot and the sauce will curdle.  Add ice to water in boiler and  simmer to maintain low temperature.  Mix egg yolks, lemon juice and salt in mixing bowl and blend thoroughly.  May use a fork to mix them.  When butter is melted, immediately add egg yolk mixture with spatula to quickly get it all in double boiler.  Whisk constantly until sauce thickens.  Make sure water not boiling in double boiler.  You want the sauce to be thick but still slightly liquid.  You may modify the recipe by adding Tabasco, paprika or cayenne pepper for a kick.

You may also convert this sauce into Béarnaise Sauce by combining 6 tbsp. of red wine vinegar, 2 tbsp. of water, 2 tbsp. of butter, 2 tsp. of minced garlic,  2 tsp. of  minced shallots, 2 tsp. of dried and 2 teaspoons of fresh parsley,  finely chopped,  in a small skillet.  Bring to a high heat and reduce liquid till almost dry.  Remove from heat and let cool for 2 minutes and add Hollandaise sauce above,  salt and pepper to taste, stirring constantly until combined.  Serve warm over steak or roast beef.

*Karen knows her husband is an outstanding chef and she says this is the best Hollandaise sauce you've ever tasted.   The Béarnaise sauce is also special and will give that meat entrée an enhanced taste.  This is an elegant touch for a dinner party.*

*3 teaspoons of fresh herbs equals 1 teaspoon of dry herbs.*

## Jalapena relish

1       doz. large Jalapeño peppers, chopped
1       lg. onion, chopped
2       tbsp.  sugar ( splenda can be used )
¼      tsp. celery seed
1/2    cup white vinegar
1/4    tsp. black pepper
1/4    cup banana yellow or red bell peppers (optional for color and flavor)

Just mix all the ingredients and stir, and you are ready to eat. For a different kind of Salsa, just add chopped tomatoes to this recipe (2 cups).

*This is another recipe from Tam and her father.*

## Melon Berry Smoothie

1   cup sliced cantaloupe
1   cup sliced honeydew
¼  cup strawberries
½  cup non-fat skim milk
¾  cup low-fat strawberry yogurt
2   cups ice

*You will find this to be a flavorful low caloric smoothie.  Delicious way to use fresh fruit or frozen fruit.*

## Party Punch

½   gallon strawberry kool aid
1   large can Hawaiian punch
1   large bottle sprite, chilled

    Mix first two ingredients together and refrigerate to chill.
Pour some of this mixture into two jello molds and freeze to make
ice rings.  When ready to serve, add remaining chilled punch and
kool aid into punch bowl.  Pour in the sprite.  Add an ice ring and
garnish with fresh fruit of your choice. (I like strawberries)  Keep the
other ice ring frozen to replenish when first one melts.

*Barbara declares this is a wonderful and delightful summer and*
*Christmas punch.  This recipe has been passed around quite a bit.*


## Pear Butter

40-50   small pears peeled and cored
1 ½     cups sugar or splenda
2       tsps. cinnamon
1/4     tsp. ground cloves

    Puree pears in a blender or processor.  Add the sugar and
spices and cook over low heat until reduced by half.  After it has
been reduced and is of smoother look, use a water bath canner and
process for 20
minutes to can.

*Tam shares this outstanding dish using fresh pears.  She feels the*
*time and effort is well worth it.*

## Pear Relish

| | |
|---|---|
| 1 | quart white vinegar |
| 2 | cups sugar |
| 2 | cups coarsely grated pears |
| 1 | tbsp. salt |
| 2 | tbsp. ground turmeric |
| 2 | tbsp mustard seed |
| 7 | cups minced onion |
| 7 | cups minced green peppers |
| ¾ | cup corn starch |
| | Water |

Heat vinegar and sugar in large pot to boiling. Add other ingredients, except cornstarch and water. Bring to a boil again. Lower heat and simmer about 20 minutes. Add enough water to corn starch to make a paste (about 1 ½ cups). Gradually stir this slowly into pot, and continue to stir until the corn starch is well cooked and relish has a clear look. Fill hot jars with the hot mixture and seal. Yields about 7 ½ pints.

*Maggie's mother made this every year and shared it with all the neighbors and her church friends.*

## Russian Tea

Put 7 regular tea bags in 8 cups of boiling water. Let steep for 5 minutes. Add 1 ½ cups of sugar or splenda, 1 tsp. ground cloves, 1 stick cinnamon, 16 oz. orange juice, 8 oz. pineapple juice, 3 tbsp. lemon juice and simmer for 30 minutes before serving.

*This would be delicious to serve with Maggie's cucumber sandwiches (see Appetizers). You are now well prepared for an afternoon tea party.*

## Tam's Pear Relish

4     qts  cored and quartered  pears
1     dozen jalapenos peppers
1     qt.  Vidalia onions
1/4  tsp. cayenne pepper
1     pint dill pickles ( hamburger chips)
1     cup salt
2     cups sugar
1 ½  tbsp. flour
1     tsp. turmeric
2     tbsp. dry mustard
1     qt. white vinegar

     If you have a grinder run all these through, but if not, process coarsely.  Add 1 cup of salt and let sit in the fridge until the next day. Drain and rinse once with cold water.  Then drain again.  In a big pot mix sugar (splenda or other), flour, turmeric, dry mustard and white vinegar.  Stir and bring to a boil for 5 minutes. Add pear mixture and bring back to a boil while stirring. Boil 5 minutes more. Put into 8 hot sterile pint jars and seal. Process in water bath for 20 minutes.

*This is another dish Tam enjoys making with her father by her side. They seem to have more in common when they are cooking to-gether.  It  has been a 'pear relish' get-together for the past 5 years. Sometimes two heads together are better than one.*

Fed by Grace

## **<u>Veggie Delight Smoothie</u>**

1     cup apple juice
1     cup sliced red apple
½    cup applesauce
½    cup sliced carrots
½    cup cucumber, peeled and sliced
2 ½  cups ice

*This smoothie tastes sweet and is a healthy addition to your diet. Quick to prepare and will  cool you down on hot days.  Delicious!*

> Any fool can count the seeds in an apple. Only God can count all the apples in one seed. — Robert H. Schuller

# Index

# Index

# Index

# Index

# Thank you

so much for the purchase of the *Fed by Grace* cookbook. Know that every penny will go to help those in need in the community being served by the Titus II women's small group of Lakeside Church. We hope you enjoy these recipes with your families and friends for years to come .

**To order more of these cookbooks:**
*Fed by Grace* cookbook can be purchased online at www.amazon.com and other places...search for us! They make great wedding, birthday or Christmas gifts!

Blessings from all of us,

   *Karen Alley, Amy Andraszek, Audrey Beals, Nancy Brooks, Damaris Callaway, Tam Cole, Kelly Clower, Doris McAfee, Maggie McClendon, Sharon Royal Minchey, April Murray, Robin Plessl, Deann Snipes, & Barbara Williams.*

LaVergne, TN USA
27 December 2010

210095LV00004B/1/P